Heaven
and Hell

Dr. David Webber

BEACON STREET PRESS
500 Beacon Drive
Oklahoma City, OK 73127
1-800-652-1144
www.swrc.com

Printed in the United States of America

ISBN 978-1-933641-65-7

Heaven and Hell

Dr. David Webber

Contents

Dedication

This book is dedicated to the lost—those who are living today without Jesus Christ. I plead with you to accept Christ and join me in Heaven for all eternity.

Heavenly Father,

I pray that some precious soul will be touched and will turn to Christ with all their heart and will say, "Yes, I believe that God has raised Jesus Christ from the dead, that He died from my sins, and He rose again for my justification" and they will make their peace with God and have forgiveness and will receive the new birth and become truly a new creature in Christ Jesus. I pray that any who read this book and do not know Christ as their personal Savior, will make that all-important decision for time and eternity. I pray in Jesus' name. Amen.

—David Webber

February 1995

Foreword

As a young man, I remember listening to David Webber on the radio. I vividly recall him starting each broadcast of the Southwest Radio Church with the words, "God is still on the throne, and prayer changes things." Even though I never personally met him, he had a tremendous influence on me. I was so impressed with his rich voice and his smooth style that I copied his mannerisms in my broadcasting career when I began working at a small market radio station at the age of fourteen. Back then, I never dreamed that one day I would serve in the same broadcasting ministry as the great David Webber.

Not only was David Webber a pioneering broadcaster, but he was also a brilliant Bible teacher. A while back, I was digging through some old audio tapes in the archives of Southwest Radio Ministries when I came across a series of David Webber programs from the mid-1990s. As I listened to him teach about Heaven and Hell, I thought that these timeless messages should be put out again for people to hear. While working on remastering the programs, I realized that putting the messages in a book would be an even better idea. You now hold in your hand the results—*Heaven and Hell.*

In this book, David does a fantastic job of reminding us that this world is not our final dwelling place. This life is not by any means the final thing. Rather, it is the brief prelude that will be followed by our eternal existence in another world.

In the life, which is to come, beyond this life, there are two possibilities as to our eternal dwelling place. Those two possibilities are Heaven and Hell. We will spend eternity either in that place of bliss called Heaven, or in an inexpressibly terrible place called the lake of fire. In *Heaven and Hell,* David Webber teaches about both possibilities in a biblically-based way that is easy to digest and comprehend.

If you are a Christian, *Heaven and Hell* will help you grow in your faith. If you are not a Christian, *Heaven and Hell* will point you to the Way to get to Heaven through Jesus Christ. Webber's clear biblical approach will strengthen your understanding and be an effective means of witness and evangelism. I believe you will learn a great deal from reading this book and be challenged to use these teachings as a starting point to a deeper study in the Word of God.

—James Collins, Staff Evangelist
Southwest Radio Ministries

Chapter 1

The Door to Heaven

I would like to ask you for a favor. I want you to join me in praying that the messages in this book will bring precious souls to Christ and cause them to think about eternity. Also, please pray that as we study these important subjects, believers will be encouraged in their faith, and God will be glorified.

I want to give you an uplift and insight into the subject of Heaven. So, we will call this chapter "The Door to Heaven." I believe you will enjoy it. Again, please pray with me that these teachings will be used to encourage people to come to Christ, the only biblical way to Heaven.

Jesus Is the Door

I want to read a Scripture from John 10, where Jesus talks about the sheepfold, and I believe He's talking about Heaven, although the word heaven does not appear:

> Verily, verily, I say unto you, He that entereth not by the door
> into the sheepfold, but climbeth up some other way, the same

is a thief and a robber. But he that entereth in by the door is the shepherd of the sheep. To him the porter openeth; and the sheep hear his voice: and he calleth his own sheep by name, and leadeth them out. And when he putteth forth his own sheep, he goeth before them, and the sheep follow him: for they know his voice. And a stranger will they not follow, but will flee from him: for they know not the voice of strangers. This parable spake Jesus unto them: but they understood not what things they were which he spake unto them. Then said Jesus unto them again, Verily, verily, I say unto you, I am the door of the sheep. All that ever came before me are thieves and robbers: but the sheep did not hear them. I am the door: by me if any man enter in, he shall be saved, and shall go in and out, and find pasture.

—John 10:1–9

Jesus Christ is the way, the truth, and the life (John 14:6). According to John 10:9, He is the door to Heaven. And I believe that when it says, "… but climbeth up some other way, the same is a thief and a robber," it is speaking about those who do not seek God but try to do things in his way by himself. So, to me, this is a description of Heaven and Jesus Christ is the door. Those who hear His voice will obtain Heaven because the Bible says that they will be saved and shall find pasture. In other words, their needs shall be supplied.

If you are a Christian, you have Heaven, the day that never ends, as your future home. In Heaven, all things will be new. It will be the day when time stands still—the Bible tells us there is coming a time when there will be no more time. We believe according to the Scriptures that God inhabits the praises of eternity. He is not bound by the dictates of time. In the words of the old song, "He the pearly gates will open so that I may enter in, for He purchased me and forgave me all my sin." Believe me, dear friends, no one will enter Heaven except through the door, which is Christ Jesus, who did purchase our redemption. He redeemed us and made us free from sin and death and the judgment that was against all who descended from Adam.

Heaven Is Indescribable

No subject should give us a greater thrill than to talk about Heaven. The Bible says, "Eye hath not seen, nor ear heard, neither have entered into the heart of man, the things which God hath prepared for them that love him" (1 Corinthians 2:9).

As we try to describe Heaven—the aspiration of the Old Testament saints, the New Testament saints, the Tribulation saints, and the Millennial saints—no earthly pen can hope to convey the completeness of joy and the fullness of peace that will be ours as Christians, born-again believers in God's New Heaven and New Earth. Having inhabited this Earth where empires crumble and fade away, where death and destruction are rampant, it is hard for us to conceive of a kind of world in which there's no death in destruction. But that day is coming.

I'm afraid the doctors will just have to play golf. They will be out of a job. And as far as construction, Jesus Christ said to His disciples, "I go to prepare a place for you. Where I am there, there you may be also." And He said, "I wouldn't have told you this if it were not true." So, we don't know whether any construction workers will be employed in Heaven. It may be all finished. We know it will not be corrupted. It will not need repairs or renovation. And someday God will reveal our heavenly inheritance, and it will be beyond human words. The false and empty shadows, the life of sin are past. God gives me mine inheritance, the land of life at last.

Yes, Jesus is the door. He is the only way that you will have a home in Heaven someday. Do you know Him?

Chapter 2

The New Heaven and a New Earth

And when the thousand years are expired, Satan shall be loosed out of his prison, And shall go out to deceive the nations which are in the four quarters of the earth, Gog, and Magog, to gather them together to battle: the number of whom is as the sand of the sea. And they went up on the breadth of the earth, and compassed the camp of the saints about, and the beloved city: and fire came down from God out of heaven, and devoured them. And the devil that deceived them was cast into the lake of fire and brimstone, where the beast and the false prophet are, and shall be tormented day and night for ever and ever. And I saw a great white throne, and him that sat on it, from whose face the earth and the heaven fled away; and there was found no place for them. And I saw the dead, small and great, stand before God; and the books were opened: and another book was opened, which is the book of life: and the dead were judged out of those things which were written in the books, according to their works. And the sea gave up the dead which were in it; and death and hell delivered up the dead which were in them: and they were judged every man according to their works. And death and hell were cast into the lake of fire. This is the second death. And whosoever was not found written in the book of life was cast into the lake of fire.

—Revelation 20:7–15

The period described here in Revelation 20 occurs at the end of the thousand-year Millennial period. Satan will be loosed from his prison and people as numerous as the sands of the sea will follow him, not satisfied with Christ Jesus. As the rebels surround Jerusalem, God, in a judgment from Heaven itself, sends down fire and slays them all. At this point, Satan is then cast into the lake of fire to join Antichrist and the False Prophet. Satan, when his armies and hoards are defeated, will be cast literally into the lake of fire, which is the second death, and he will be a permanent exile from the presence of God and all the redeemed.

After that, the unsaved dead are raised from the dead in what is commonly referred to as the second resurrection. The Bible says in Revelation 20:5, "Blessed and holy is he that hath part in the first resurrection." This is when the believers are raised to life eternal with Christ. But then notice one of the saddest verses in all the Book of Revelation. The Bible says in Revelation 20:15, "And whosoever was not found written in the book of life was cast into the lake of fire."

The Purging Fire

Then God seeks to purge even the physical Earth and heavens of any evidence of sin. He does this by sending a fire so intense that it melts the elements with fervent heat and burns the Earth. Now, we remember also God has atomic fire. He has fire that is so intensely hot—something we've never experienced on this planet. But God's fire can either illuminate, as in the case of Moses' burning bush, or it can destroy and burn up, as we read in Isaiah 66 and in 2 Peter 3:

> But the day of the Lord will come as a thief in the night; in the which the heavens shall pass away with a great noise, and the elements shall melt with fervent heat, the earth also and the works that are therein shall be burned up. Seeing then that all these things shall be dissolved, what manner of persons ought ye to be in all holy conversation and godliness, Looking for and hasting unto the coming of the day of God, wherein the heavens being on fire shall be dissolved, and the elements shall melt with fervent heat?
>
> —2 Peter 3:10–12

When this happens, God will have rid the universe of the last vestige of man's pollution through sin, and every Christian will enter the most thrilling glory that God has prepared, a New Heaven and a New Earth. The heavens will not be unclean in God's sight. The New Earth will have no curse, no sin, no death, and destruction.

The Former Shall Not Be Remembered

One of the first inklings that God gives us about the divine inheritance for us is found in the Old Testament book of Isaiah. Isaiah 66:1 says, "Thus sayeth the Lord, the heaven is my throne and the earth is my footstool." In other words, God's headquarters are in Heaven, the third heaven above our atmosphere, and of course, the part of heaven, the second heaven, where there is no gravitational pull as we feel it upon this Earth, and up about a hundred miles above the canopy of this Earth. "Heaven is my throne and earth is my footstool."

We're told in Isaiah 65:17, "For, behold, I create new heavens and a new earth: and the former shall not be remembered, nor come into mind." We don't know exactly when this will come about. Many people think it will be toward the end of the millennial reign. Some think at the beginning of the millennial reign, or during the millennial reign. And I do know, I don't think you could be dogmatic about it. We tend to believe it will be during the day of the Lord or during the millennial reign or toward the end of it. Nevertheless, God's promise standeth sure.

Modern Beliefs About Heaven

Have you ever heard someone say, "The devil made me do it?" Three years ago, only half the population, fifty-two percent could have made such a claim. But this Gallup poll shows that these days, two-thirds of Americans, sixty-five percent, believe in the devil. At the end of one of the most contentious years in recent memory marked by natural disasters, sensational trials, Olympic skulduggery, and a nasty election campaign, seventy-three percent believe there is a Hell, up from sixty-seven percent in 1981 and sixty-six percent in 1968.

On the positive side, nine in ten Americans think there is a Heaven. Seventy-nine percent believe in miracles and seventy-two percent in angels. However, two other supernatural beliefs have gained some support over the past four years, with twenty-eight percent now believing in communication with the dead, up ten points from 1990, and twenty-seven percent believing in reincarnation, up six points. Only astrology at twenty-three percent has lost ground, down by two points.

Belief in Heaven is high across the demographic spectrum. Most skeptical are those with post-graduate education. But even here, three-quarters believe. At the other extreme are those who consider themselves members of the religious right, about thirteen percent of adult Americans, one hundred percent are believers.

Belief in Hell reveals some interesting divergences. Seventy-five percent of those under age sixty-five are believers. Above that age, the figure drops sharply to sixty-four percent. Four in five southerners—eighty percent—believe, but only sixty percent of Westerners. Even politics is a factor. Eighty-four percent of those who voted for George Bush in 1992 say there is a Hell, but only sixty-five percent of Ross Perot and Bill Clinton voters agree. This trend is also reflected in presidential approval. Sixty-six percent of Clinton supporters are believers. Among his detractors, eighty percent believe in Hell. In only two categories is a real disparity between men and women, and in both instances, men are less apt to believe. Eighty-six percent of women believe in miracles compared with seventy-one percent of men. The angel gap is thirteen points with seventy-eight percent of women and sixty-five percent of men calling themselves believers.

So, that is a result of a recent Gallup poll, which I thought you would find of interest.

More About Heaven

I wonder if you can grasp the full significance of this verse. "For, behold, I create new heavens and a new earth: and the former shall not be remembered, nor come into mind" (Isaiah 65:17). The marvelous and beautiful things of God's headquarters—God's Heaven—are so wonderful we forget about this dusty old Earth in which things die and crumble to decay. It will be so wonderful, so breathless in sight and activity, it will literally occupy all our thoughts. We will not even remember this old world we call planet Earth. It simply will not come into our minds.

Can you imagine such tranquility, such peace of mind? There will be no homesickness for the old things of Earth, such will be the dazzling splendor of this New Earth, and the New Heavens are no longer tarnished by the evil traffic of the prince of the power of the air.

Scriptures indicate that we will be the same person, having the same soul as we have now, redeemed by the blood of the Lamb. Our names will be written in the Book of Life of the Lamb slain from the foundation of the world, and we will have a new glorified body. Praise God! The characteristics of this new body will no doubt bear a relationship to our former body, much the same as the qualities of Christ's resurrection body, born to His same pre-resurrection body.

The Bible tells us when we accept Christ as Savior and Lord, we too are spiritually a new creation. "Therefore if any man be in Christ, he is a new creature: old things are passed away; behold, all things are become new" (2 Corinthians 5:17). The new birth, the birth that is from above, is spiritual, and of course it will make us new. All things are passed away. Behold, all things are become new, and that will be true of us redeemed by the blood of the Lamb. We will be created new in all things, untouched, unmarred by sin. We will truly be new creatures in every respect once we have received our new glorified bodies.

And I saw a new heaven and a new earth: for the first heaven and the first earth were passed away; and there was no more sea. And I John saw the holy city, new Jerusalem, coming down from God out of heaven, prepared as a bride adorned for her husband. And I heard a great voice out of heaven saying, Behold, the tabernacle of God is with men, and he will dwell with them, and they shall be his people, and God himself shall be with them, and be their God. And God shall wipe away all tears from their eyes; and there shall be no more death, neither sorrow, nor crying, neither shall there be any more pain: for the former things are passed away. And he that sat upon the throne said, Behold, I make all things new. And he said unto me, Write: for these words are true and faithful.

—Revelation 21:1–5

In Revelation 21:1–2, we read about new heavens, a new Earth, and a new Jerusalem. Here will be a place finally without corruption. No decay, no rust. Many people think that silver won't rust, However, rust, which is iron oxide, also has its counterpart, even in silver oxide and silver sulfide. All metals today corrode in one way or another.

For example, for every hour of plane flight time in Vietnam, it required twenty-five man-hours of anti-corrosion maintenance. NASA and the military together spend $10 billion per year fighting corrosion damage. Of course, you know what happens to your priceless silver if you don't polish it. And God tells us in James 5:3, "Your gold and silver is cankered; and the rust of them shall be a witness against you."

The government of the Millennium will be a theocracy. A theocracy is a government in which God is recognized as the supreme ruler; His laws are taken as the laws of the state, and he will rule the nations with a rod of iron, according to Isaiah 2.

In the Millennium, there will be three classes of people. Number one, all the saved of Israel alive at the end of the seven-year Tribulation period. Number two, all the saved of the gentiles alive at the end of the seven-year Tribulation period. Number three, the believers who have died before the Rapture. These resurrected saints will have positions of responsibility in the Millennium (see Matthew 19:28; Luke 19:12–77).

Chapter 3

Life in the Millennium

But the day of the Lord will come as a thief in the night; in the which the heavens shall pass away with a great noise, and the elements shall melt with fervent heat, the earth also and the works that are therein shall be burned up. Seeing then that all these things shall be dissolved, what manner of persons ought ye to be in all holy conversation and godliness, Looking for and hasting unto the coming of the day of God, wherein the heavens being on fire shall be dissolved, and the elements shall melt with fervent heat? Nevertheless we, according to his promise, look for new heavens and a new earth, wherein dwelleth righteousness.

—2 Peter 3:10–13

I ended the last chapter by beginning a discussion about life in the Millennium and what it will be like. In the Millennium, living believers will be able to marry and be given in marriage. The women will reproduce and have children. I believe there will be a population explosion like in the days of Noah (Genesis 6:1). This will be a population explosion such as we have never seen in our lifetime.

These children born in the Millennium will be given an opportunity to accept Christ or reject Him at the end of the Millennium when Satan is loose for a little season. Life in the Millennium will be one of peace (Isaiah 11:6–9), happiness, (Isaiah 11:6–9; Revelation 20:3), and long life and health (Isaiah 33:24; 65:20). The New Heavens and the New Earth follow the Millennium chronologically. Thus, believers who through acceptance of Christ are now new creatures will be completely fulfilled in all of God's glory in the New Heavens and the New Earth.

We recall the relationship between Christ and His saints is revealed in Christ's high priestly prayer in John 17. His intercession in Gethsemane when He prayed, "Father, I will that they also, whom thou given me, be with me where I am, that they may behold my glory, which thou has given me." There will be no need of hospitals, nor will there be pain and sorrow, no heart disease, arthritis, diabetes, cancer, headaches, and nervous tension. It will all be forever gone. We will have a new body, a glorified body, and it will no longer be sick. And of course, we know there will be a new Jerusalem.

The Location of the New Jerusalem

Where is this new city? Some suggest New Jerusalem will be suspended over the Earth, which I have long believed according to Psalm 48. And we read in Revelation 21:1–2, "And I saw a new heaven and a new earth: for the first heaven and the first earth were passed away; and there was no more sea. And I John saw the holy city, new Jerusalem, coming down from God out of heaven, prepared as a bride adorned for her husband."

It is important to remember that this new golden city, Jerusalem, will not be identical to the one on this present Earth. We read in Revelation 21:10, "And he carried me away in the spirit to a great and high mountain, and shewed me that great city, the holy Jerusalem, descending out of heaven from God." God is revealing to John, the author of this inspired book of Revelation, that great city, Jerusalem, descending out of heaven. I believe, because of several scriptures, that this new city of Jerusalem is suspended over the Earth as John sees it in the future. Why do I believe that? Simply because the Bible tells us the men who are saved shall walk in the light of the New Jerusalem.

Today, we walk in the light of the sun. It doesn't rest upon the Earth. The sun revolves almost 93 million miles away from this planet. I don't think the New Jerusalem will be that far, but since the Bible also tells us in these catastrophic days, the heaven and the Earth, the sun and moon, will flee away, that the New Jerusalem will go into perhaps geosynchronous orbit and it will provide light for the Earth, which the sun accomplished prior to the end of days.

So, we suggest the new city Jerusalem is suspended like a great golden chandelier over the Earth, as John sees it in the future apocalypse. One of the interesting aspects of these new things is that while God chose to reveal to us in one single verse the creation of New Heavens and a New Earth, there are at least twenty-five verses which describe in great detail the New Jerusalem.

You know, it's hard for man to fathom the characteristics of this new city, Jerusalem, an eternal city without a temple. And of course, there will be a temple in the Millennial Earth, and I believe Jesus Christ will be the builder. But here in this new city, Jerusalem, there will be no need for a temple, for Christ will be the temple and He will be the light thereof. The entire city will be like a temple, and we will worship, such worship as perhaps we've never known on this Earth. It will be a vast cubicle, holy of holies, wherein God dwells (Revelation 21:16).

There Will Be No Darkness

Since there will be no sin and our conversation and thoughts will be holy, we will be dwelling with God in that holy city. The Bible tells us there will be no darkness there. Christ will be the light that illumines that city. And personally, I believe the light will reach out even to this Earth, for Jesus said in John 8:12, "I am the light of the world. He that follow with me shall not walk in darkness, but shall have the light of life."

With sin gone, and with the saints being in the physical presence of God, His light will be our light and there will be no night there. The Bible says in Revelation 21:25, "For there shall be no night there."

Other Things That Will Not Be in Heaven

There will be no tears in Heaven. There will be no more pain in Heaven. No more sorrow. No crying in Heaven. There will be no death in Heaven. Here is God's wonderful promise to every Christian who has placed his faith and trust in Him. Revelation 21:4 reads, "And God shall wipe away all tears from their eyes; and there shall be no more death, neither sorrow, nor crying, neither shall there be any more pain: for the former things are passed away." What a glorious transformation when His blessed face I see. No more pain and no more sorrow. Oh, what glory that will be.

My dear friends, we need to realize that no man can look upon God's face until we are redeemed. You must be transformed by the power of the indwelling Christ and saved and sealed with the Holy Spirit. Then your eyes will be spiritual eyes that can see things that are hidden from you today.

Chapter 4

Welcome to Your New Home

I knew a man in Christ above fourteen years ago, (whether in the body, I cannot tell; or whether out of the body, I cannot tell: God knoweth;) such an one caught up to the third heaven. And I knew such a man, (whether in the body, or out of the body, I cannot tell: God knoweth;) How that he was caught up into paradise, and heard unspeakable words, which it is not lawful for a man to utter.

—2 Corinthians 12:2–4

Our vocabulary, as Paul tells us, is inadequate to describe all the wonders and beauties and glories that will be Heaven. We can't do it justice. We realize that, but we try to give you little glimpses of what we do know from the Word of God.

For the scripture foundation, we read from Revelation 22:

And he shewed me a pure river of water of life, clear as crystal, proceeding out of the throne of God and of the Lamb. In the midst of the street of it, and on either side of the river, was there the tree of life, which bare twelve manner of fruits, and yielded her fruit every month: and the leaves of the tree were for the healing of the nations. And there shall be no more curse: but the throne of God and of the Lamb shall be in it; and his servants shall serve him: And they shall see his face; and his name shall be in their foreheads. And there shall be no night there; and they need no candle, neither light of the sun; for the Lord God giveth them light: and they shall reign for ever and ever.

—Revelation 22:1–5

Welcome to your new home. All that we hope for will be realized and, I think, much, much more. Have you ever experienced the thrill the first time you walk into your new home? It is an event of happiness, contentment, and fulfillment. Over the years, however, that feeling fades away, especially when the roof needs repairing, or the furnace needs replacing. But my dear friends, in Heaven that initial joy will continue throughout all eternity. There will be no disappointments in Heaven.

Let's examine some characteristics of God's Heaven.

The Light of the Lamb

The Bible says in Revelation 21:22–23, "And I saw no temple therein: for the Lord God Almighty and the Lamb are the temple of it. And the city had no need of the sun, neither of the moon, to shine in it: for the glory of God did lighten it, and the Lamb is the light thereof." The sunlight will be dazzling—the glory of God and the Lamb. There will be no sunburn. The city had no need of the sun, neither of the moon to shine in it for the glory of God did lighten it and the Lamb is a light thereof.

There will be no darkness. Now, we don't understand that because when we have night, across the world it's daytime. But God is the light, and the light will be supreme, no shadows, no darkness. No need for candles or light bulbs or even sunlight, for the Lord God will be by His very presence light supreme, and He will illuminate this New Jerusalem and the New Earth.

The River

The river that proceeds from the throne of God is a pure river, clear as crystal. This is the river of Paradise with its fountainhead being God and the Lamb, Paradise restored. While the streams of Earth are polluted, this river of life is pure and clear as crystal.

The Tree of Life

The tree of life that was found in the Garden of Eden before man ever sinned is restored to this beautiful city. The tree is in the street and on either side of the river. This tree of life has twelve varieties of fruit, yielding each month its fresh crop. My father used to say, "By the time you'd gotten tired of apples, here comes oranges. By the time you're tired of oranges, pears or grapefruit or bananas or whatever." There will be twelve kinds of fruit, one every month, that you can enjoy to the full. And there is a bonus. The leaves of the tree will be for the healing of the nations. And it is never barren.

You may recall in Genesis 2:9 that out of the ground the Lord God made to grow every tree that is pleasant to the sight or to be desired. But of course, by disobeying God's law, Adam caused sin to enter the world. Now this beautiful tree of life in the New Jerusalem has healing in its leaves, forgiveness to all who believe. And there's no temptation, no more curse. Satan is relegated to the lake of fire and is no longer present. The devil is in permanent exile, and the curse has been removed as God promised (Revelation 22:3).

The City of Gold

The city will be as transparent gold (Revelation 21:18). This may be hard to imagine as nothing on Earth can presently duplicate a pure gold that is clear and transparent as glass. Yet God showed John a sight of this new city, New Jerusalem, which he could only describe as having streets of gold so clear and transparent that it resembled glass.

Dr. J. Dwight Pentecost points out some things that will be in the eternal city of New Jerusalem. Number one, a life of fellowship with him. Number two, a life of rest. Number three, a life of full knowledge. Number four, a life of holiness. Number five, a life of joy. Number six, a life of service. Number seven, a life of abundance. There will be no homeless there. They will be at home in the presence of God and the Lamb, around the throne of His splendor. Number eight, a life of glory. And number nine, a life of worship—worship such as we've never known on this planet. What a marvelous revelation of our new home. What a marvelous promise.

Will You Be There?

The gates of it shall not be shut at all by day, nor shall there be any night there (Revelation 21:25). Nothing and no one shall enter in but they which are written in the Lamb's Book of Life. You know, in Revelation 20 we see the books are open for the judgment of the unsaved dead. They are brought back in a corruptible state—a horrible thought to contemplate. But also, because God is just, the Lamb's Book of Life will be open at the Great White Throne judgment. I do not believe a single individual who stands before the Great White Throne will be found in the Book of Life, for no unsaved person will be in Heaven. There will be nothing there to defile this heavenly kingdom. All things will have passed away and all things will be new.

What greater promise is there than that found in 1 John 3:2? There, the Bible says, "Beloved, now are we the sons of God, and it doth not yet appear what we shall be: but we know that, when he shall appear, we shall be like him; for we shall see him as he is." We shall be like Him for all eternity. How long is eternity? Eternity is forever. We can't conceive of this either. In this world, man must either decide to accept Christ as personal Lord and Savior or, by sinful indecision, reject him. Based upon that decision, he destines himself either for God's forgiveness and an eternity in Heaven or for God's judgment and an eternity in the lake of fire. Try to imagine that this Earth upon which we dwell is nothing but sand. Now try to imagine that a little bird could fly through space from a distant planet to ours and carry back with him a tiny grain of sand.

That the round trip would take a thousand years. Now imagine how long it would take for that little bird to carry away this entire Earth, a grain of sand each thousand years. The time required for all this would be but a moment in comparison to eternity.

Where will you spend eternity? Will it be in the places that God has prepared for them that love Him? Or will it be a place of darkness, disorder, and torment? A place where permanent exile of the devil and his angels will be confined to some wandering star, some black hole, some literal lake of fire.

My friends, it's all in the Bible. The Bible says that you, made in the likeness and image of God, must decide where you will spend eternity. I pray it will be in the presence of God and the Lamb, in heavenly places that God has prepared for all those who love Him.

Chapter 5

Oh, Hear the Angel Voices

Our discussion about Heaven and Hell would be incomplete if we didn't spend some time talking about angels. The subject of angels is of great interest in popular culture. Just look around. Angels are everywhere.

Angels in Song

We sing about angels in gospel songs. For example, the familiar refrain to Fanny J. Crosby's song, "Blessed Assurance," speaks of "...angels descending bring from above, echoes of mercy, whispers of love." However, we sing about angels more often in popular songs. An estimate has been made that one in every ten popular songs refers to angels in some form. That may have even been truer in the 1950s, which I remember very well. It is kind of a nostalgic period for me. Songs such as "Teen Angel," "Earth Angel," "Johnny Angel," "Angel Eyes," and "I'm Living Right Next Door to an Angel," all topped the charts.

Angels in Movies and Television

Movies, of course, have featured angels, both old and new. Classics such as *Angel on my Shoulder*, *The Bishop's Wife*, and *It's a Wonderful Life*, had angel themes. In the summer of 1994, one could find *Angels in the Outfield* at Angel Stadium helping the Anaheim Angels baseball team.

Angels have become a kind of media phenomenon. You can hardly watch television these days without some mention of angels. One of the highest rated television series in recent years was "Highway to Heaven" featuring an angel as its hero. The series "Touched by an Angel" is also very popular.

Today, angels are the frequent topic of talk shows. They appear often as an element in advertisements and commercials. For example, an NBC television special on angels aired in May 1994 under the heading "Angels: The Mysterious Messengers." It scored such a rating success, it was re-broadcast in July. After the first airing, some seventeen thousand people called in to request a tape of the show. A book with the same title was released by Valentine in August, and several other angel specials were planned by NBC in the fall of 1994.

Angels in Books

One of the foremost writers about angels is Sophy Burnham. Her book, *A Book of Angels*, has had thirty-six printings, with more than seven hundred thousand copies in print. *Where Angels Walk* was on the bestseller list for eighteen weeks and had half a million copies in print after fifteen printings. *Angel Letters* has had twelve printings and two hundred forty-five thousand copies in print. While these books have made the top of the secular book selling charts, other books on angels have been regulars on Publishers Weekly religious bookseller list, as well as on lists published by the Christian Book Seller's Association.

Angels Are Part of Our Everyday Lives

It seems that the popularity of angels does not wane. Paintings and sculptures of angels have been displayed in major museums and galleries around the world for centuries. Many of these depict Bible scenes. But today, angels have moved beyond being players in Bible stories to being symbols of beauty, grace, strength, mercy, wisdom, hope, innocence, peace, truth, and guardianship.

Obviously, angels are a part of our vocabulary. We eat angel food cake and delicate angel hair pasta. We put angel fish in our aquariums. Of course, we named a city for angels, Los Angeles, as well as the longest uninterrupted waterfall in the world, Angel Falls in Venezuela. We say that a person who barely scrapes by does so "on a wing and a prayer." We say that children look like "angels" when they're sleeping, that people with beautiful voices "sing like angels," and that those who help others are "angels of mercy."

Angels seem to have a role in the folklore of many cultures, including many that do not draw the basis of their belief system from the Bible. To the Balinese, angels are depicted as winged mermaids. To the Vikings, they're called *Valkyries*. The Greeks called them *horae*, the Persians *fereshteh*, and the Hindus *apsaras*. In Malaysia, freckles are referred to as angel kisses.

Do You Believe in Angels?

Apparently, we not only talk and sing about angels, paint them, study them, and tell stories about them, but we actually believe in them. A recent *Time Magazine* poll indicated sixty-nine percent of Americans believe in angels, while only twenty-five percent do not. The young especially seem to have a growing belief in angels. A Gallup youth survey conducted in the spring of 1992 found that seventy-five percent of American teenagers ages thirteen to seventeen believe in angels. This figure was up from sixty-four percent in 1978. During the intervening years, teen belief in other supernatural and paranormal events actually declined.

What exactly do we believe about them? Well, when a *Time Magazine* poll asked five hundred Americans which description best described the angels a person believed in, the answers were broken down as follows. Higher spiritual beings treated by God with special powers to act as his agents on earth, fifty-five percent; the spirits of people who have died, fifteen percent; an important religious idea, but merely symbolic, eighteen percent; and the fourth category, figments of the imagination, seven percent. In the same poll, subjects were asked if they had ever felt an angelic presence in their lives. Some thirty-two percent said yes and thirty-five percent said no. About a third apparently were unsure. Maybe so, maybe not. When asked if they believed in the existence of fallen angels, or devils, forty-nine said yes and forty-five, no.

What we can conclude from polls such as these is that although angels are very popular, we attach very different meanings and beliefs to them. What we can also conclude is that the rate of interest in angels has increased dramatically in the last decade. Literally thousands of accounts of activities of angels have been recorded in recent months and years. That calls us to ask several questions:

» Why this great interest in angels?

» Why an apparent increase in angelic activity?

» Why are people apparently more willing to talk about their experiences with angels?

» Are today's angels the same as those of the Bible?

I strongly believe that the Lord God wants us to be informed about the supernatural realm, but He also wants us to have accurate information. So, for the next chapter, I want to look at what the Bible has to say about angels.

Chapter 6

Angels in the Bible

> I beheld till the thrones were cast down, and the Ancient of days did sit, whose garment was white as snow, and the hair of his head like the pure wool: his throne was like the fiery flame, and his wheels as burning fire. A fiery stream issued and came forth from before him: thousand thousands ministered unto him, and ten thousand times ten thousand stood before him: the judgment was set, and the books were opened.
>
> —Daniel 7:9–10

How many angels are there? Well to answer that question, I want to look at a glimpse of Heaven as seen by the prophet Daniel. In Daniel 7, we have a picture of God's throne and the innumerable angels who are God's messengers and who do God's bidding. Notice that the Bible says, "… thousand thousands ministered under him and ten thousand times ten thousand stood before him" (Daniel 9:10). So obviously, there are millions of angels.

In my research, I have found some amazing information about angels. Angels are mentioned more than three hundred times in the Scriptures. The writers of both the Old and New Testaments do not explain the origin of angels. They simply assume their existence. The good angels of Heaven are called elect angels in the Scriptures (1 Timothy 5:21). In other words, when one-third of the angels fell and followed Lucifer in rebellion against God and his administration, the remainder, or two-thirds of the angels, chose to follow God, and they became his elect angels.

Angels in the Old Testament

The appearance of angels is recorded thirty-two times the first five books of the Bible, the Torah; thirty-seven times in the books that detail the development of the kingdom of Israel in the books Joshua, Judges, 1 and 2 Samuel, 1 and 2 Kings, 1 and 2 Chronicles, and the oldest book of the Bible, Job; frequently in the one hundred fifty chapters in the book of Psalms; by all of the major prophets with the exception of Jeremiah; and by the minor prophets Hosea and Zechariah. The Old Testament writers did not feel it necessary to offer formal proof that angels exist. They simply assumed them to exist and to be involved with men at the directive of God.

Angels in the New Testament

The gospels of the New Testament are also filled with reference to angels. They are mentioned six times in the book of Acts. Paul wrote of angels in many of the epistles attributed to him, and James and Peter also referred to angels. The book of Revelation alone has at least sixty-five references to angels. Among those many references, angels are seen by John in relationship to the book with seven seals (Revelation 5:2–5); standing on the four corners of the Earth, holding back the four winds of the Earth (Revelation 7:1); and ascending from the east, having the seal of the living God to seal the 144,000 (Revelation 7:2-3).

The angels were very active in the life of Jesus. From what He said and taught about them; it seems obvious that Jesus believed what most Jews in that day believed—that angels are real, they are present all around us, and that angels are assigned to individual human beings. Jesus had the authority to call many legions of angels to His aid (Matthew 26:53). Jesus is recorded as saying of those who confess His name, He will confess before the angels. And those who deny Him, He will deny before the holy angels in Heaven (Luke 12:8-9).

The angels rejoice when one sinner repents, according to Luke 15:10. Angels see the face of the Father in Heaven. And therefore, Jesus says we should not despise one of these little ones (Matthew 18:10). The reapers of the harvest at the end of the age are angels (Matthew 13:39). When Jesus returns, He will come in the glory of His Father with all the holy angels (Mark 8:38). Angels escort saints to God's presence at the time of their death (Luke 16:22). The same chapter reflects that the rich man died, and he woke up in Hell. He was in torment. So, we might say conversely, that wicked angels escort those who die without Christ to the lower regions of the Earth.

To the surprise of many, angels are not readily associated with harps, music, or halos in the Scriptures. They do not lazily look out their heavenly windows on human affairs or sit passively on clouds. These elements have been added by artists throughout the ages. Apparently, from the holy Scriptures, angels are very active. They are in continual worship around the throne of God (see Revelation 5:11–12 and Isaiah 6:3). They are also active in the affairs of men.

Someone might ask the question, do angels have personality? Yes. Personality is not defined by who man is, but by who God is. God is the originator of all personality. He is the archetype of all personality in the creatures He has made, including angels. Now, angels were created, we can assume, before God made man in his likeness and image. Angels are immortal. We do not read that angels die. Of course, from other scriptures we understand that angels have these major aspects to their personality: intelligence, emotion, and will.

Angels have a desire to learn, communicate with speech, and have a revelatory knowledge of God's plan for this world (Matthew 28:5, Revelation 10:5–6, and Revelation 7:1–18). The wise woman of Tekoa in 2 Samuel 14:20 refers to the king as wise, according to the wisdom of the angel of God. What is it that angels know? Perhaps the chief thing that angels know is the nature of God. They have a vital, intimate, face-to-face relationship with God. They dwell in His presence and surround his throne. It must be a very large area, bigger than a football field, because they have so many in attendance according to Daniel 7 and Revelation 5. And they worship him continually. I believe that is the way in which we will be like angels—we will not die, and we will worship God continually.

The elect angels also know the reality and nature of the fallen angels. They observed Lucifer's rebellion, the fall of Lucifer, and the fall of those who rebelled with him. They know how to counteract these demons in a way that no human being can grasp fully. They're not only able to discern the devil's traps and snares, but they are one hundred percent capable of defeating the devil and his demons at every turn. And remember, one angel will cast Lucifer into the bottomless pit and chain him up for a thousand years (Revelation 20:2).

Chapter 7

The Ministries of Angels

The word angel comes from the Greek word *angelos,* which means messenger. The Hebrew word is *malach,* which also means messenger. Of course, you might think about Malachi, the last book of the Bible, whose name means "God's messenger." Other Bible words for angels, both Hebrew and Aramaic, have been translated as the mighty, sons of God, ministers, and servants.

Augustine differentiated between the nature of angels and the office, or work, of angels. He said this: "'Angel' is the name of their office, not of their nature. If you seek the name of their nature, it is 'spirit'; if you seek the name of their office, it is 'angel': from what they are, 'spirit,' from what they do, 'angel.'" It is in the function or office of speaking or giving messages that we find a number of angels at work and a number of important missions fulfilled by God's angelic beings.

We need to note of the outset that the word *angelos* can refer to both human beings and spirit beings in the Greek. A pastor or human message bearer might also be called *angelos.* Some of the references in the book of Revelation may be to pastors or to human messengers. This is especially true for chapters two and three, the messages to the churches. Later in Revelation, however, the messages are more clearly linked to spirit being messengers, angels.

Let's look closer at the ministries of angels:

Angels Are Preachers

And I saw another angel fly in the midst of heaven, having the everlasting gospel to preach unto them that dwell on the earth, and to every nation, and kindred, and tongue, and people, Saying with a loud voice, Fear God, and give glory to him; for the hour of his judgment is come: and worship him that made heaven, and earth, and the sea, and the fountains of waters.

—Revelation 14:6–7

The angels in Revelation 14 have a definite preaching mission. Here we see them preaching the gospel. Up to that time in the last days, however, we have no mention of angels preaching directly to men or women.

Angels Are Proclaimers

On several occasions, angels in the Bible issue announcements or proclamations, both to individuals and to all of mankind. For example, in Revelation it is an angel that announces, "Babylon is fallen, is fallen, that great city, because she's made all nations to drink of the wine of the wrath of her fornication" (Revelation 14:8).

Angels Are Interpreters

In several places in God's Word, we find angels filling the role of interpreter. As John begins his Revelation of Jesus Christ, he tells us that Jesus sent and signified it by His angel to His servant John, who bore witness of the Word of God and to the testimony of Jesus Christ to all things that John saw (Revelation 1:1). Later in the book of Revelation, we read how an angel interprets the mystery of the woman and the beast with seven heads and ten horns (Revelation 17:7).

An angel also interpreted the vision that Zechariah received from the Lord (Zechariah 1:18–19). Perhaps nowhere in the Scriptures are angels more closely linked to prophecy than in the book of Zechariah. In only thirteen chapters, angels are mentioned in the book of Zechariah twenty times, with frequent reference to "the angel who talked with me" (Zechariah 2:3 and Zechariah 4:1).

Angels Are Messengers

Repeatedly in the holy Scriptures, we find passages in which angels came to individuals with specific messages. Several of them were to Abraham and his family. One of these messages was given to Hagar, Sarah's handmaid. Sarah had given Hagar to Abraham so that he might have an heir when it appeared she would not be able to bear children. When Hagar discovered she was pregnant, she began to show disrespect to Sarah. Sarah, of course, in turn dealt harshly with Hagar, and Hagar fled into the wilderness.

Subsequently, the Angel of the Lord found Hagar by a spring of water in the wilderness. And he said, "Hagar, Sarah's maid, where have you come from and where are you going?" And she answered, "I am fleeing from the presence of my mistress, Sarah." The Angel of the Lord said to her, "Return to your mistress and submit to herself under her hand." Then the Angel of the Lord said to her, "I will multiply your descendants exceedingly so that they shall not be counted for multitude." Then the Angel of the Lord said unto her, "Behold, you are with child, and you shall bear a son. You shall call his name Ishmael because the Lord has heard your affliction. He should be a wild man. His hand shall be against every man and every man's hand against him. And he shall dwell in the presence of his brethren" (Genesis 16:7–13).

Of course, you can see it is a family argument between the Jews and the Arabs and the Palestinians. On the surface, we might conclude we need to retract our statement that God does not send angels to assist those who will be disobedient, but that isn't the case here. God is not sending His angels to help those who are rebellious or outside His redemption. Hagar is a part of Abraham's family.

Yea, whiles I was speaking in prayer, even the man Gabriel, whom I had seen in the vision at the beginning, being caused to fly swiftly, touched me about the time of the evening oblation. And he informed me, and talked with me, and said, O Daniel, I am now come forth to give thee skill and understanding. At the beginning of thy supplications the commandment came forth, and I am come to shew thee; for thou art greatly beloved: there-fore understand the matter, and consider the vision.

—Daniel 9:21–23

In Daniel 9, we met the angel Gabriel. Daniel is told twice that Gabriel has come to give him understanding. Then, of course, Gabriel proceeds to give to Daniel the meaning of the seventy weeks, one of God's major timetables for Israel.

It was Gabriel who told Zacharias about the birth of John the Baptist who would be a prophet to prepare the way for the Lord (Luke 1:1–25). Then he told Mary about the Lord Jesus Christ being conceived by the Holy Spirit in her womb (Luke 1:26–38).

The birth of Christ was announced by angels. The angel said to the shepherds, "For unto you is born this day in the city of David a Saviour, which is Christ the Lord" (Luke 2:11). Then the angels sang for joy, "Glory to God in the highest, and on earth peace, good will toward men."

Chapter 8

The Unseen World

There is an unseen world—a world our hands cannot touch, our eyes cannot see, our ears cannot hear. In this unseen world, a battle is raging—a battle between God and Satan. Though we cannot see this world or its combatants, they are there just the same. The agents of the devil today are some of the best-educated men and women who are even leaders of their own professions. The late Bishop James Pike was recognized as a leading theologian in championing the modernistic doctrines, yet he was convinced that he talked with his dead son through a spirit being.

In practically all nations today, illiteracy is being abolished. Almost every child receives a high school education, and an increasingly large percentage go to college. But never has there been such a revival in spiritism and Satanism. It is no longer illogical to believe in witches and evil spirits. These are popular subjects to explore.

God said that in these last days the devil would flood the world with fallen angels and demons. According to Revelation 12:9, the day is coming when the devil himself and all his hordes will be cast out from Heaven forever and confined to this Earth, and by the increase of spirit activity, we know that this day spoken of by God is near at hand.

Some may be reticent to accept the proposition presented in the Scriptures and embraced by millions today that there is a personal devil and there are spirit beings traversing the heavens and invading the Earth. But God Himself declares it. First Corinthians 15:39–40 says: "All flesh is not the same flesh: but there is one kind of flesh of men, another flesh of beasts, another of fishes, and another of birds. There are also celestial bodies, and bodies terrestrial: but the glory of the celestial is one, and the glory of the terrestrial is another."

Terrestrial Life

The Scriptures divide terrestrial life into four main divisions: men, beasts, fishes, and birds. God created each of these four divisions with a body to function and operate within the environment in which it was placed. If men had never seen a bird, they would scoff at the idea that there existed a form of animal life that could fly in the air. If men had never seen or heard of a fish, they would find it difficult to believe a form of animal life could live by breathing under water, or that this species could be frozen and then brought back to life.

Celestial Life

The Apostle Paul went one step further to declare that apart from the four main divisions of terrestrial life, there was celestial life.

The Word of God further declares that this celestial life was created to operate and function within all the environments found throughout the universe. Therefore, these spirit beings have bodies that will endure the extremely cold temperatures that exist in outer space.

They also probably must live in places where there is no oxygen; and according to the biblical description, they must travel at speeds approaching or exceeding the speed of light. There is no known life form on this planet that can exist in such environments; yet we know from the Bible that such celestial beings are in existence, and the spirit activity in evidence today indicates that they are also here on Earth.

There is but a thin veil between the spirit world and the world of the natural man. Spirits desire to possess the bodies of men, and some men and women seek after spiritual contact with the powers of the air. Often the dimension of the spirit and the dimension of the flesh merge and become visible to each other. Abraham talked with the angels who visited him, and their bodies looked like those of men (Genesis 18). Daniel conversed freely with Gabriel (Daniel 8–9). The night that Christ was born, the shepherds near Bethlehem saw a multitude of the heavenly host (Luke 2:8–20).

Classifications of Angels

The heavenly hosts faithful to God are made up of seraphim (God's watchers over the creation—Daniel 4); cherubim (the guardians of the third Heaven—Genesis 3:24); the angels (God's faithful servants and messengers throughout the cosmos—Psalm 68:17;

Isaiah 66:15); and the archangels (God's princes who rule over the angels—Jude 9; Daniel 12:1).

As far as we know, there were never more than three archangels. Although Michael is the only archangel identified as such in the Bible, most theologians agree that Scripture indicates there are two others—Gabriel and Lucifer. However, Lucifer fell from his exalted position when iniquity was found in him. It may be concluded from scriptural information available that each archangel ruled over one-third of the angelic host. Revelation 12:3–4 seems to lend validity to this interpretation, "And there appeared another wonder in heaven; and behold a great red dragon ... And his tail drew the third part of the stars of heaven. ..."

The great red dragon is identified in Revelation 12:9 as Satan, and stars are often used in the Bible as symbolic of angels. Thus, it becomes evident as we search the Scriptures that Satan, when he was the bright and shining one named Lucifer, ruled over one-third of the heavenly bodies and he had under his dominion one-third of the angelic hosts.

The Bible says in Isaiah 14:12 that Lucifer was called the "son of the morning," indicating that he was one of the first to be created. In Ezekiel 28:12 he is said to have been full of wisdom and perfect in beauty. In Ezekiel 28:13–17 we discover further that he was full of brightness. The name Lucifer in the Hebrew means "the bright and shining one." But, as we find also in Ezekiel 28 and Isaiah 14, because of his exalted position he became vain and proud. He sought to exalt his own throne above all the stars of God, the angelic host. He knowingly and consciously rebelled against God.

He was the first sinner, the first rebel, the first apostate. Instead of "the wise one," he became a liar and a murderer. Instead of the son of the morning, he became the devil, our adversary. Instead of the bright and shining one, he became the serpent, that old dragon, the king of the demons, the prince of darkness.

Satan used his great wisdom to lie and deceive the angels under his dominion. They followed him in his rebellion against God to conquer the universe. He is still using his perverted wisdom and wickedness to deceive the world today. The fallen angels, his loyal subjects, are invading Earth to prepare the way for Satan's false messiah, the Antichrist. This appears to be the reason for the alarming rise in spiritism, witchcraft, and Satanism. It is a sign that we are living in the terminal generation. Satanic activity is a sign that the time of sorrows, known as the Tribulation period, is about to break upon the world.

> And I saw three unclean spirits like frogs come out of the mouth of the dragon, and out of the mouth of the beast, and out of the mouth of the false prophet. For they are the spirits of devils, working miracles, which go forth unto the kings of the earth and of the whole world, to gather them to the battle of that great day of God Almighty.
>
> —Revelation 16:13–14

The intensity of spirit activity in the last days is described in Revelation 16. This is John's description of demons spreading over the face of the Earth. We are living at the time of the beginning of this spirit activity today.

The Final Battle Has Already Begun

The final battle of this age between the forces of Satan and the forces of God is described in Revelation 12, "And there was war in heaven: Michael and his angels fought against the dragons: and the dragon fought and his angels, And prevailed not; neither was their place found any more in heaven" (Revelation 12:7–8). John saw, by revelation, the final and deciding battle, but the war began millennia ago when Satan declared in his heart: "I will ascend into heaven, I will exalt my throne above the stars of God: I will sit also upon the mount of the congregation, in the sides of the north: I will ascend above the heights of the clouds; I will be like the most High" (Isaiah 14:13–14).

Being born again into the Kingdom of God, Christians are active participants in the spiritual war between God and the devil. Paul wrote in Ephesians 6:10–12:

> Finally, my brethren, be strong in the Lord, and in the power of his might. Put on the whole armour of God, that ye may be able to stand against the wiles of the devil. For we wrestle not against flesh and blood, but against principalities, against powers, against the rulers of the darkness of this world, against spiritual wickedness in high places.

A recent news article discussed the rise of Satan worship. The article stated in part:

> What democracies in general, and America in particular, most

lack is belief in the devil, argued Denis deRougemont a quarter century ago. But if few Americans outside the Bible Belt were willing then to give the devil his due, today tens of thousands across the U.S.—some of them middle-class adults with advanced university degrees—are dabbling in Satanism, witchcraft, voodoo, and other forms of black or white magic ... a good deal of the experimentation results from plain blind faith in satanic power, which sometimes produces macabre acts of violence and sex. ...

This news article related specific crimes of murder and sex mutilation so horrible that I am reticent to offend my readers with descriptions of them. The article continued, "... most of those convicted or suspected of such killings have demonstrated some kind of involvement with the Church of Satan."

The Scriptures contend that there are many "wiles" of the devil; the growing power of Satan in the world manifests itself in many forms. *Time Magazine* has reported on the increasing number of witches and participants in occult worship in the world:

As 250 fellow worshipers formed a circle around them and chanted the ancient Hindu mantra "om," the bride and bridegroom watched the priest and priestess, and their helpers conjure into their midst the gods and goddesses of the four elements—air, water, earth and fire. ... The bizarre ceremony, performed in a scruffy campground outside Demotte, Ind., was not some stunt but a modern pagan "handfasting," or wedding. It was one of the highlights of the Third Annual Pan Pagan Festival, a four-day conclave that brought together a witch's brew of 325 paganists, occultists and witches from 26 states and Canada. ... The festival, organized by a group called the Midwest Pagan Council, reflected what some religious leaders find to have been a rather rapid spread of neo-paganism around the country over the past decade. J. Gordon Melton, an Evanston, Ill., Methodist minister who heads the Institute for the Study of American Religion, reckons that there may be as many as 4,000 practicing pagans today.

According to reports, occult groups are massing and forming colonies across the world. In the United States, such organizations are buying property and even in some instances, incorporating as cities or townships, or taking over existing cities and townships. One of the most noted of these is in Antelope, Oregon. The July 4, 1982, edition of the *Sunday Oregonian* reported:

About 6,000 followers of Bhagwan Shree Rajneesh were joined by their spiritual teacher ... as a five-day festival began about 20 miles southeast of Antelope. The festival coincides with the first anniversary of the Rajneesh Foundation International's purchase of the 64,000-acre Muddy Ranch. It also is a celebration of Guru Purima, the traditional Eastern observance in which devotees gather with their masters. ... To accommodate the red-clad visitors attracted to the festival, three tent cities—close to 2,000 tents in all—have been set up on the ranch. The compounds are named for Buddha, Socrates, and Zarathustra. ... The tent dwellers come from across the globe. Australians, Germans, Brazilians, and many other nationalities are represented in the throngs that line the country road each afternoon as Rajneesh takes his daily spin in one of his Rolls-Royces.

According to various newspaper reports regarding this movement, wives are leaving their children and husbands, and husbands are deserting their mates, to live in this commune type of free love society. The head of the movement, Rajneesh, projects a father-God figure to his followers, a savior who promises love, peace and relief from all responsibilities and stress. He is just one of the thousands of false christs appearing on the world scene today. Even schools, churches, and so-called youth rehabilitation agencies are using occult meditation practices to open the minds of young people to demonic possession. Jesus said of the end of the age: "For many shall come in my name, saying, I am Christ; and shall deceive many" (Matthew 24:5).

Satan is making his final effort to forever annex Earth to his kingdom. This battle, and life-and-death struggle during the coming Tribulation, will determine the future of the heavens and the Earth. We know the outcome from God's Word, but the beginning of the struggle signifies a time of great tribulation ahead. Christians should put on the whole armor of God so that they may stand against the wiles of the devil (Ephesians 6:13–18).

Chapter 9

Spirit Activity in the Heavens

The Scriptures are replete with references concerning the teeming activities of the spirit world in the heavens. We read in Hebrews 12:22 that the angels who inhabit heavenly places are innumerable. All angels are not of the same order. In Scripture we read of seraphim, cherubim, angels (some serving God and some serving the devil), archangels, principalities, powers, thrones, dominions, fallen angels, spirits in prison, demons, seducing spirits, sons of God, morning stars, watchers, and elders.

Perhaps the most complete picture of the relationship of the spirit world to the throne of God is found in the fourth chapter of Revelation. During the course of the Revelation of Jesus Christ, John was caught up into the presence of God, and he saw the throne of God. There is a literal Kingdom of God, and like every kingdom, God's Kingdom has a throne.

And round about the throne were four and twenty seats: and upon the seats I saw four and twenty elders sitting, clothed in white raiment; and they had on their heads crowns of gold. And out of the throne proceeded lightnings and thunderings and voices: and there were seven lamps of fire burning before the throne, which are the seven Spirits of God. And before the throne there was a sea of glass like unto crystal: and in the midst of the throne, and round about the throne, were four beasts full of eyes before and behind. And the first beast was like a lion, and the second beast like a calf, and the third beast had a face as a man, and the fourth beast was like a flying eagle. And the four beasts had each of them six wings about him; and they were full of eyes within: and they rest not day and night, saying, Holy, holy, holy, Lord God Almighty, which was, and is, and is to come.

—Revelation 4:4–8

The scene which John describes around the throne of God depicts the higher echelons of God's governmental administration. The king of any monarchical type of government is always the center of supreme authority. From the king, authority in administrative rule is delegated to cabinet members, prime ministers, judges, and so on. The four angelic creatures before the throne of God are called beasts because they have the appearance of certain beasts in the animal kingdom. The root word in the Greek text for beasts in this Scripture is *zoon,* indicating that the English translators were correct in their interpretation. These beasts rest neither day nor night. They are full of eyes, indicating they are ever watching.

The Watchers

The four watchers, by their very nature, indicate that they watch over the whole creation, including lower life forms. This is also substantiated by Revelation 4:11: "... for thou hast created all things, and for thy pleasure they are and were created."

The twenty-four elders are upon the seats. The word "seat" is still used to refer to delegated and administrative governmental authority, as when politicians "run for a seat" in Congress.

The fourth chapter of Daniel affords some light into the administrative duties of the watchers.

> I saw in the visions of my head upon my bed, and, behold, a watcher and an holy one came down from heaven. ... Let his [meaning Nebuchadnezzar's] heart be changed from man's, and let a beast's heart be given unto him; and let seven times pass over him. This matter is by the decree of the watchers, and the demand by the word of the holy ones: to the intent that the living may know that the most High ruleth in the kingdom of men, and giveth it to whomsoever he will, and setteth up over it the basest of men.
>
> —Daniel 4:13, 16–17

One of the watchers, one of the four beasts, gave Nebuchadnezzar a beast's heart: the king ate straw in the field like an ox. The holy ones demanded that Nebuchadnezzar's kingdom be taken from him, and the watchers fulfilled the decree.

The Cherubim

In addition to the watchers, there are elite angelic guardian forces of God called cherubim. In Genesis 3:24, we read that God placed cherubim around the Garden of Eden to keep man from eating of the "tree of life" and living forever in a godless and lost condition. Cherubim were placed over the mercy seat, indicating their protective position around the throne of God.

The Seraphim

Another rank of the angelic order is the seraphim. We read of them in Isaiah 6:6–7:

> Then flew one of the seraphims unto me, having a live coal in his hand, which he had taken with the tongs from the altar. And he laid it upon my mouth, and said, Lo, this hath touched thy lips; and thine iniquity is taken away, and thy sin is purged.

The root word for seraphim means "serpent." They have six wings, like the watchers before God's throne, but their role in God's government appears to be more of a priestly nature. They have charge over the altar of God in Heaven from which the burning coal came to take away the iniquity of Isaiah.

Angels

Another order of the spirit world is the angels. Angels are messengers and servants of God who serve throughout the universe, and they are so great in number that they cannot be counted. There is nothing said in Scripture about angels having wings. Their celestial travel is associated with the chariots of God. We read in Psalm 68:17 that "the chariots of God are twenty thousand, even thousands of angels. ..." Isaiah 66:15 says, "For, behold, the Lord will come with fire, and with his chariots like a whirlwind, to render his anger with fury, and his rebuke with flames of fire."

Angels are described in appearance as looking like men; the Bible tells us that men are a little lower than the angels. Angels eat food. We know this because Abraham served the angels who visited him a hearty meal. We read in Psalm 78:24–25: "And ... rained down manna upon them to eat, and had given them of the corn of heaven. Man did eat angels' food. ..."

Archangels

The last identifiable members of the angelic order are the archangels, possibly the most important and trusted members of God's Kingdom. They are the only ones of God's angels mentioned by name. Since the fall of Lucifer, there are only two of these, and their names are Gabriel and Michael. We read in Jude 9: "...Michael the archangel, when contending with the devil he disputed about the body of Moses." Gabriel is mentioned by name in Daniel 8:16 and other scriptures, and in Daniel 12:1 the archangels are called princes. Michael is called a prince of God, and therefore it follows that Gabriel is also a prince. The identification of the archangels as princes gives them throne rights in the Kingdom of God, and the Word indicates that Gabriel and Michael each rule over one-third of God's Kingdom and each commands one-third of the angelic host. This completes the roster of the spirit world within the universe who are faithful to God.

Chapter 10

The Origin of Satan

Now, I want to identify the members of the spirit world who are in rebellion against God. At the head of the "Kingdom of Darkness" is Lucifer, who became Satan and the devil. We know from Scripture that God did not create a devil, but that one of the exalted ones of God's Kingdom became ambitious and because of pride, determined to elevate his throne above the throne of God. We read in Isaiah 14:12–13:

> How art thou fallen from heaven, O Lucifer, son of the morning! how art thou cut down to the ground, which didst weaken the nations? For thou hast said in thine heart, I will ascend into heaven, I will exalt my throne above the stars of God: I will sit also upon the mount of the congregation, in the sides of the north.

We read in verse 14 that Lucifer said in his heart that he would become like God.

How did Lucifer conceive such an ambition? What prompted it? To understand what changed this angelic being from a faithful servant of God into a prince of evil and darkness (the god of this world), we must go back to the dawn of creation.

In the Beginning

We know the angels, like man, were a direct creation of God (Hebrews 1:6). However, nothing is said of their creation within the six days of creation in Genesis 1. Their creation must date back to the dawn of creation mentioned in Genesis 1:1: "In the beginning God created the heaven and the earth." Angels are called the "sons of God" because they were created beings.

Originally, it would appear that the spirit world fell into two categories—the sons of God (the angels), and the first created, "the morning stars." Both orders were created prior to the creation of the world. We read in Job 38:4, 7: "Where wast thou when I laid the foundations of the earth? ... When the morning stars sang together, and all the sons of God shouted for joy?"

Let us keep in mind, as we trace the tragic career of Satan, that God rewards faithful service. To the redeemed from humanity, God has promised that some will sit on thrones, some will judge, and some will sit in heavenly places with Christ. There are many rewards and degrees of authority and responsibility to be determined at the Judgment Seat of Christ. If this be true of the future estate of the saved from among men, and indeed it is true, then it follows that the same rule of rewards for service could also apply to the angels.

From the higher angelic order, which was created in the beginning, the morning stars, it appears that many were selected to fill positions of leadership in God's Kingdom. Let us now follow the career of one particular member of this angelic order, the one who eventually became Satan, our adversary.

Satan's Career

Lucifer was originally a "son of the morning" (Isaiah 14:12). He advanced to the status of a trusted cherubim, a member of the heavenly guard. We read in Ezekiel 28:14, "Thou are the anointed cherub that covereth; and I have set thee so. ..."

From the status of a cherubim, a position which he must have filled most admirably Satan advanced to the status of a seraphim, a priest in the temple of God in Heaven. We read in Ezekiel 28:14: "... thou wast upon the holy mountain of God; thou hast walked up and down in the midst of the stones of fire."

Probably the next promotion that Lucifer received was an appointment to be a watcher before the throne of God. Because of the similarity in appearance, a watcher is apparently a higher order of seraphim. Of the four watchers described in Revelation 4:7, one has the face of a lion, a watcher over the wild animal kingdom; one has the face of a man, a watcher over the human race; and one has the face of an eagle, a watcher over the bird kingdom. We notice that there is no watcher over the reptiles, and the reason is given in Habakkuk 2:14, "... O Lord, thou hast ordained them for judgment; and, O Mighty God, thou hast established them for correction. ... And makest men as the fishes of the sea, as the creeping things, that have no ruler over them?" God's watchers have the appearance of that part of the life of creation over which their responsibility lies. Satan appeared in the Garden of Eden in the form of a snake, and one of his names is "the dragon," or "that old serpent." Satan's promotion left a vacancy within the order of watchers which has never been filled, probably as the result of a curse that God put on the creeping and crawling things because of Satan's sin.

The fifth and last promotion of Lucifer was doubtless to the rank of an archangel. Only the archangels are named, and Lucifer was Satan's name when he fell. "How art thou fallen from heaven, O Lucifer. ..." Lucifer had a throne, and only archangels were given thrones because of their princely positions. "I will exalt my throne above the stars of God ..." (Isaiah 14:13). Satan commanded an army of one-third of the angelic hosts, and only archangels are said to command the armies of God (Revelation 12:3–9).

There is no doubt that Lucifer was the most intelligent and beautiful angel in God's entire universe. He was found perfect in service (Ezekiel 28:15). God recognized Lucifer's capabilities and rewarded him accordingly, yet he became ambitious and would stop at nothing to extend his own kingdom (which God had given him) over the entire universe.

The Forces of God vs. the Forces of Satan

With the rebellion of Lucifer, the spirit world was divided into two opposing forces. According to Ezekiel 28:18, Satan and his angels hold fortified territories in the heavens from which they wage war against the Kingdom of God and Earth. This is the subject of Paul's warning in Ephesians 6:11–12:

> Put on the whole armour of God, that ye may be able to stand against the wiles of the devil. For we wrestle not against flesh and blood, but against principalities, against powers, against the rulers of the darkness of this world, against spiritual wickedness in high places.

Never have visible manifestations of this unseen war been so evident as in our day. A few years ago, the American Medical Association issued a warning against people becoming involved in the occult movement that is sweeping across the world. This supreme medical authority warned that both mental and physical health could be destroyed. There is only one power in heaven and in Earth that can overcome these evil agents of Satan, and that is the power of the blood of Jesus Christ. First John 5:5–6 says: "Who is he that overcometh the world, but he that believeth that Jesus is the Son of God? This is he that came by water and blood. ..."

Chapter 11

The Satanic Conspiracy

The account of Lucifer being cast down from Heaven to the Earth in Isaiah 14 is given from a prophetic viewpoint. Lucifer, the original revolutionary, planned to take over the Kingdom of God. We read in the Bible of war in Heaven. But at some time in the future, Lucifer, who became Satan, will be cut down to the Earth. We read of this coming event in Revelation 12:12: "Therefore rejoice, ye heavens, and ye that dwell in them. Woe to the inhabiters of the earth and of the sea! for the devil is come down unto you, having great wrath, because he knoweth that he hath but a short time."

The Satanic Kingdom

Jesus indicated in Matthew 24:6–7 that at the end of the age, when Satan would try to set up his kingdom on Earth, there would be wars and rumors of wars; nation would rise against nation, and kingdom against kingdom. This prophecy foreshadows revolutions and world wars to weaken the nations. Part of this satanic plan, according to Ezekiel 38–39, would be the rise of communism, an anti-God power in Russia. Then, according to Ezekiel, Russia would align with four Muslim nations and invade the re-founded nation of Israel. Also, according to the eleventh chapter of Daniel, and other prophecies in Revelation, the armies of all nations will become involved in the Middle East.

The Antichrist

It will be at this time that Satan will set up a world governmental system and appoint his own ruler over it. This world dictator is called "the Beast," or the Antichrist. Under his administration, which will govern all the Earth, everyone in the world will be commanded to worship Satan as the supreme god of the universe.

We read of the establishment of Lucifer's kingdom on Earth in Revelation 13:4–8:

> And they worshipped the dragon which gave power unto the beast: and they worshipped the beast, saying, Who is like unto the beast; who is able to make war with him? And there was given unto him a mouth speaking great things and blasphemies; and power was given unto him to continue forty and two months. And he opened his mouth in blasphemy against God, to blaspheme his name, and his tabernacle, and them that dwell in heaven. And it was given unto him to make war with the saints, and to overcome them: and power was given him over all kindreds, and tongues, and nations. And all that dwell upon the earth shall worship him, whose names are not written in the book of life of the Lamb slain from the foundation of the world.

The Battle of Armageddon

It will be toward the end of the brief reign of this satanic world dictator that the armies of all nations will be gathered into the Middle East to prevent the return of Jesus Christ. We read from Zechariah 14:14:

> Behold, the day of the Lord cometh ... I will gather all nations against Jerusalem to battle ... Then shall the Lord go forth, and fight against those nations ... And his feet shall stand in that day upon the mount of Olives, which is before Jerusalem on the east. ...

A more detailed description of the return of Jesus Christ with the armies of Heaven to destroy Satan's dictator, along with the armies of the world, is given in Revelation 19 and Revelation 16:11–14. The downfall of the entire satanic conspiracy is also described in 2 Thessalonians 2:7–9:

> For the mystery of iniquity doth already work: only he who now letteth will let, until he be taken out. of the way. And then shall that Wicked be revealed, whom the Lord shall consume with the spirit of his mouth, and shall destroy with the brightness of his coming: Even him, whose coming is after the working of Satan with all power and signs and lying wonders.

The Restrainer

The only thing that is preventing the establishment of Satan's government over all nations is the Holy Spirit, who is witnessing to the world today, through Christians, about Jesus Christ and His power to save. My understanding of the promise of God recorded in 1 Thessalonians 4:13–18 is that Christians will be taken out of the world before the time of great tribulation spoken of by Jesus in Matthew 24:21. Then Satan's world government, under the Antichrist, will be instituted upon Earth.

Chapter 12

Servants of Satan

We are admonished by the Scriptures to resist all the wiles of the devil, because Satan uses many devices to add souls to his kingdom. God also tells us in His Word about Satan and his angels, and the Bible mentions demon possession repeatedly. "Demons" in the English language is sometimes rendered "devils," meaning agents of the devil.

The scope of eschatology reflects an increase in demonic and fallen angelic activity in the latter years. In the past decade many books on increasing satanic manifestations by noted Christian theologians and authors have poured from the presses. These books warn that the devil today is indeed going about like a roaring lion, seeking those whom he may devour (1 Peter 5:8).

I would like to quote from just a few of these:

Satan's master stroke of policy is to divert our minds from inquiry concerning his true character and the methods by which he governs his kingdom. His resources are so varied and his modes of operation so elastic that it is extremely difficult to determine the bounds of his authority. Sometimes he employs the vehicle of darkness to blind the minds of those who do not believe, lest the light of the Gospel of the glory of Christ should dawn upon them (2 Cor. 4:4). And sometimes, unto those who do believe the Gospel, he transforms himself into an angel of light, that thus, by bewildering, he may delude them into his snares (2 Cor. 11:14).

Is it primitive superstition, just so much nonsense—or are there really evil spirits in the world around us? In this book I say there are such spirits, and I present some of the evidence. I show some of the subtle ways in which they manifest themselves. Sometimes they even materialize ... they can and do utilize psychological principles, while at other times their influence is essentially in the spiritual realm. The fact is that ALL their activities are intrusions into the spiritual, for that is the ultimate reality. The devil and his demons know that if one method of attack fails, they will use another. They have patience, they have skill, and they have hatred—hatred of God and hatred of man because he is God's crown of creation. Today they have come out into the open. They have initiated an assault in ways that a generation ago would have seemed unthinkable.

The Devil has changed his public image. He's no longer a comical character with pointed ears, a pitchfork and hooves. Satan has exposed himself. Today he's the leading character in bestselling novels and successful films. People worship him in elaborate black masses. Do-it-yourself books on Satanism are invading suburbia. Courses on the Occult and Astrology are offered in some school districts.

Witchcraft and Satan worship spread throughout campuses and cities. In America, a so-called civilized country, people are involved in weird rites and rituals. We are all part of an unseen conflict in the world and within ourselves. ... Consider what is said about this clever character, Satan. Anyone who has dominated history as he has cannot be ignored, especially in these days. To do so may be at the peril of your very life.

So that we may know our enemy, let us identify the powers and rulers of darkness whom Satan is using to corrupt the masses even as he did in the days of Noah.

Astrologers

Satan operates on the theory that every man has his price, and he offers something for everybody. Perhaps the most inoffensive and seemingly harmless of the agents of Satan are the astrologers. Movie stars, millionaires, congressmen, kings, and men of renown in all areas of politics, economics, the arts, and even religion, depend upon their horoscopes for guidance in daily affairs. Yet, the Bible does not have one good word to say about an astrologer or the false science of astrology. Isaiah 47:13–14 says, "Let now the astrologers, the stargazers, the monthly prognosticators, stand up, and save thee from these things that shall come upon thee. Behold, they shall be as stubble; the fire shall burn them; they shall not deliver themselves from the power of the flame. ..."

It is also evident from the first, second, fourth, and fifth chapters of Daniel that astrologers are the agents of Satan, and a rise in astrology always precedes demon possession and the moral disintegration of a nation. Astrology can be traced back to Babel, and even further back to the antediluvians. Paul wrote in Romans 1:23 that God condemns all those who change the glory of God's creation into "an image made like to corruptible man, and to birds, and four footed beasts, and creeping things" (symbols in the zodiac). The apostle says that God gives such deceived people up to vile affections, crime, and sexual perversions. Astrology precedes moral disintegration and satanic destruction. It is no coincidence, in light of national moral decay, that astrology is booming. In 1953, only about one hundred newspapers carried horoscope columns. Twenty years later, approximately two thousand newspapers carried daily horoscopes, and there were almost two hundred thousand professional astrologers. In other nations the percentage of the population that reads their daily horoscope and patronizes astrologers is as follows: Britain, sixty-six percent; France, fifty-three percent; Germany, sixty-three percent.

Sorcery

The root word for "sorcery" in the Greek text means "pharmacy" or "drugs" in English. Sorcerers have always used drugs (called magic potions) to cause visions, or as we would say today, hallucinations. Sorcerers, and all those who engage in traffic with sorcerers, are condemned in God's Word. Jeremiah 27:9, Isaiah 47:9, Daniel 2:2, and many other Old Testament scriptures identify sorcerers as agents of Satan. Elymas, the sorcerer of Acts 13, is called a "child of the devil (v. 10). But it is remarkable that the sorcerers predicted for the last days in Revelation are most strictly defined in the Greek as merchants of drugs (*Young's Analytical Concordance*). Revelation 9:13–21 depicts the widespread use of drugs in the last days, causing murder, sexual depravity, robbery, demon possession, and devil worship. We read in Revelation 18:23 that all nations will have a serious drug problem just before Christ returns. The reduced penalty for marijuana possession in our own country is another example of Satan working behind the scenes.

An example of drug addiction causing demon possession was carried in *Decision,* in an article entitled "Exit the Monkey Demon." The young man whose personal testimony of demon possession was recorded in the article said: "I am convinced that anyone who has taken LSD (the same applies to other drugs) for any amount of time is possessed by some principle of evil, and the only one who can cast out demons is Jesus Christ." Sorcerers, or drug merchants, are sixth on the list of those for whom is reserved the hottest fires of Hell (Revelation 21:8). Drugs are the devil's medicine for the last days, and certainly one of the wiles of the evil one to corrupt the world.

Witches

Not too long ago, it was estimated that there were at least five thousand witches in New York, ten thousand in Los Angeles, and in the entire United States there were one-half as many witches as clergymen. In view of the declining membership in the churches of many of the larger denominations and the rise of witchcraft, it may be just a matter of time until witches outnumber clergymen. In England, France, Germany, and other nations in Europe, witchcraft is reported to be even more widespread than in the United States.

God identifies witches in the Bible as agents of Satan, and the Israelites were commanded to put a witch to death (Exodus 22:18). The acceptance of witches as the more respectable members of the new occult society testifies to the fact that Satan is tightening his grip upon the world in preparation for the coming struggle. He will then make his final effort to exalt his kingdom of darkness above the Kingdom of God.

Prognosticators

Predictions by Jeanne Dixon, Sibyl Leek, Maurice Woodruff, Edgar Cayce, and a host of other prognosticators, clairvoyants, and seers have filled the newspapers for the past several decades. Jeanne Dixon is consultant to some of the most prominent figures in the arts and politics, and she is one of the best-known people in the world today. Her widespread popularity and common identifiability testifies to her acceptance as a credible prophet. She uses astrology, the crystal ball, ESP, and visions—the whole occult ball of wax that is condemned over and over in the Bible. Yet she wrote in her book *The Call to Glory:* "It is my belief God has given me a gift of prophecy for His own reasons. ... God talks to me. I know then, beyond all doubt, that the channel is coming directly to me from the Divine, the Lord our God."

Of all the modern prognosticators, Miss Dixon claims the highest percentage of accuracy, approximately eighty percent. But what of the approximate twenty percent which she misses? Are these of God also? If so, then God would be a liar. A true biblical prophet to whom God gave insight into the future by the Holy Spirit was never wrong but was one hundred percent accurate— this is the test of a true prophet of God (Deuteronomy 18:20–22).

Prognosticators are identified in Isaiah 47:13 with those who are of Satan and who lead the unwary away from God's Word for wisdom concerning those things which are coming upon the Earth. Yet it is probable that most people read the forecasts of modern prognosticators more than they consult the "... more sure word of prophecy ... a light that shineth in a dark place ..." (2 Peter 1:19). In her more recent visions, Jeanne Dixon predicts a glorious world in the near future through reincarnation, but she overlooks the coming judgments of the Great Tribulation.

Spiritists

Spiritists, also called mediums, are those who claim contact with the world of the departed dead through the medium of familiar spirits. Spiritists have become popular in these last days along with all the other deceivers of Satan. In 1967, a well-known medium, Arthur Ford, was on a television show with the late Bishop James Pike, and millions across the nation were involved in this "trip to the spirit domain." Through the televised experience of these two men, countless adherents to spiritism were gained. The religious posture of Bishop Pike deceived many, even some who professed Christ as Lord and Savior. Spiritism continues to gain acceptance by an increasing number of people.

God identifies those who seek to contact the dead through familiar spirits as in league with the devil. Isaiah 8:19–22 says:

> And when they shall say unto you, Seek unto them that have familiar spirits, and unto wizards that peep, and that mutter: should not a people seek unto their God? for the living to the dead? ... And they shall look unto the earth; and behold trouble and darkness, dimness of anguish; and they shall be driven to darkness."

Demons

Besides the fallen angels of Satan's kingdom, there are demons. Satan is nowhere in the Bible ascribed to have the power to create life in any form; therefore, it may seem a mystery as to where demons originated. Due to the fact that demons have no bodies and desire the bodies of the living (humans or animals), some believe that they are the spirits of the half-angels and half-humans that resulted from the union between the fallen angels of Genesis 6:2 and woman on Earth. Their bodies were destroyed in the Flood, but their spirits continued to live. Regardless of their origin, demons are identified in the Bible as real, and as servants of Satan; until the day of their judgment by Jesus Christ (Matthew 8:29). Satan is called Beelzebub, the prince of demons (Matthew 12:24).

People become demon-possessed when they place themselves on Satan's ground, and this is evidently why many on drugs fall prey to these agents of the bottomless pit. The existence of demons was classified by the scientific community as superstition, but demon possession has become so evident today that few bother to deny their existence. The motion picture *The Exorcist,* and other like movies, dramatized before millions the reality and torture of demon possession. Demon possession is referred to in 1 Timothy 4:1: "Now the Spirit speaketh expressly, that in the latter times some shall depart from the faith, giving heed to seducing spirits, and doctrines of devils."

One college professor boldly dressed up like the devil to propose what we consider satanic programs to his students. Quoting from the November 7, 1982, edition of *Savannah News-Press:*

When professor Newtol Press dons his plastic horns, he may suggest that all people in the world should look alike or that some poor people should be sterilized. He plays devil's advocate in an attempt to goad his students into thought, and officials at the University of Milwaukee say his bioethics course is popular. "I'll suggest sterilizing welfare mothers, killing the elderly to save money," Press said. "Many of the students were a little perplexed, a little disoriented to find out they would actually have to solve problems like this. But they say they enjoy thinking and this is one of the few courses that enables them to do that." Press, 51, decided to play the role of the devil's advocate about five years ago when he and other teachers were looking for a way to get their students to do more than just repeat information.

The Bible predicts an influx of demons upon the world from the bottomless pit in the last days to possess those who have turned from God and accepted Satan as their master (Revelation 9:1–12). Demonic activity today bears evidence that we are living in the last days.

Apostates

Perhaps the most effective agents of the devil are the apostates who stand in the pulpits of the churches. An apostle is one chosen by God to declare that God's Son, Jesus Christ, has come in the flesh. An apostate is one chosen of Satan to deny that Jesus Christ has come in the flesh: "For such are false apostles, deceitful workers, transforming themselves into the apostles of Christ. And no marvel; for Satan himself is transformed into an angel of light" (2 Corinthians 11:13–14). Every preacher today who denies that Jesus Christ is the only begotten Son of God, and denies His atoning death on the cross, is an agent of Satan working to prepare the way for Antichrist: "And every spirit that confesseth not that Jesus Christ is come in the flesh is not of God: and this is that spirit of antichrist, whereof ye have heard that it should come; and even now already is it in the world" (1 John 4:3).

Down through the Church Age, few ministers, either in the Roman Catholic Church or non-Catholic churches, have had the courage to make such a blasphemous charge against God's Son.

Yet today, the majority in Protestant churches do it boastfully and unashamedly every Sunday morning. According to recent clerical polls (*Christianity Today*), over fifty percent of the seminary graduates believe that Jesus Christ was only a man, nothing more. The increasing number of blatant apostates occupying positions as pastors and church officials testifies that Satan is swiftly preparing the world for Antichrist.

Trying the Spirits

Christians are admonished in 1 John 4:1: "Beloved, believe not every spirit, but try the spirits whether they are of God. ..." So, it is possible for you to try the spirits. By Bible definition, astrologers, witches, drug pushers, prognosticators, spiritists, demons, apostates, and a host of others in the growing occult movement of our day, are being used by Satan in an attempt to prevent the glorious return of our Lord Jesus Christ.

Satanists are spreading over our nation offering sacrifices and drinking blood in their damnable black masses. Evidence is growing that the Earth is under a severe satanic attack, both from within and from without. The night of the Tribulation must be near at hand. Christians, who are of the day, should be diligent, observing the signs of the times and holding up the Lord Jesus Christ as the only name given among men whereby they must be saved.

Chapter 13

The Door to Hell

I want to address the subject of Hell. Now you might say, "I want to go to Heaven. Why are you talking about Hell?" Simply because there's thousands of people out there who are destined to go to Hell and it's a fearful place.

We know that Jesus Christ came that man born of Adam might have life and more abundant life. God is not willing that any should perish, that any should go to Hell. But since you're made in the likeness and image of God, you are a creation of choice and the only way to Heaven is Jesus Christ who said, "I am the way, the truth, and the life." God will only accept you if you believe and receive His anointed Son, the Lord Jesus, as your personal Savior and wash away your sins in the precious blood of Calvary.

> Therefore hell hath enlarged herself, and opened her mouth
> without measure: and their glory, and their multitude, and their
> pomp, and he that rejoiceth, shall descend into it.
>
> —Isaiah 5:14

The Bible indicates in Isaiah 5:14 that hell will enlarge herself. Hell will be enlarged because so many people will end up there. Hell will also set on fire the foundations of the Earth. Personally, I believe that the reason many volcanoes that have been extinct for hundreds of years are suddenly beginning to erupt again, like Mount St. Helen and volcanoes in Hawaii and other places, is because we are in the last days. We read in Deuteronomy 32:22, "For a fire is kindled in mine anger, and shall burn unto the lowest hell, and shall consume the earth with her increase, and set on fire the foundations of the mountains." That could be the ring of fire of volcanic activity again coming into catastrophic outburst. Notice that the Bible says that Hell will "set on fire the foundations of the mountains." Volcanoes, of course, are high places like the mountains.

The Night That Never Ends

Hell is a place of eternal suffering. At the end of the Millennial period of a thousand years, many people, as numerous as the sands of the sea, will join with Satan in the final revolt against God and His people. This extremely vast army will represent the dregs of civilization. Even after a thousand years of perfection on Earth, these people are still determined that they can achieve a world far better than God in His infinite wisdom.

How often in the past has man sought to take things in his own hands and boast of his accomplishments? Accomplishments that were possible only because God permitted them because God is longsuffering and not willing that any should perish. Not even the abundance of the thousand-year Millennium period will be good enough for them. And personally, I believe that Jesus Christ will reign a thousand years over the nations of the Earth to show man that the only way to deal with sin is through the precious shed blood of Jesus. But not even the abundance, when the curse is removed for the thousand-year Millennium, will suffice to make all people believers and subservient to the great King of Kings and Lord of Lords.

Unfortunately, there will be people who will be born during the Millennium who will not learn their lesson from the events at the end of the Tribulation period, when the Antichrist and the False Prophet seek to literally annihilate Israel. It is at that time that God intervenes and wipes out the combined army of 200 million demons (Revelation 9). The aftermath of Armageddon will leave a bloodbath that will cover one hundred eighty-five miles of Israel, according to Revelation 14:20.

It is at this time that Antichrist and the False Prophet are cast into the lake of fire. An angel casts Satan in the bottomless pit for a thousand years and binds him with a great chain. At the end of the Millennium, Satan is on the march again. Apparently, a thousand years in the bottomless pit will not reform him. Then for a brief season the divine restraint will be relaxed. One purpose of this is to provide one last and supreme demonstration of the appalling wickedness of the non-believing human heart. Man's heart is deceitful and desperately wicked. Who can know it? Only God.

With all his men, more numerous than the sands of the sea, one would think Satan would make some dent in his invasion of the area around Jerusalem Were it not for God, who is in control, he could and would. But something unusual occurs. God causes a spectacular phenomenon to take place. Here's how the Bible describes it:

> And they went up on the breadth of the earth, and compassed the camp of the saints about, and the beloved city: and fire came down from God out of heaven, and devoured them.
>
> —Revelation 20:9

Fire came down and devoured them. They were decisively and immediately burned up. Just think of it. Multiple thousands, perhaps millions, of people, in a flashing moment are suddenly consumed by God's fire that comes thundering down from heaven.

Now we know that Satan brought sin into the world. It began in Genesis 1:31, which reads, "And God saw every thing that he had made, and, behold, it was very good." It was after this that the fall of Satan must have taken place. It was Satan who caused the fall of the human race in the Garden of Eden (Genesis 3). And God, of course, gave His judgment upon Satan, and upon Adam and Eve. Satan's power was second only to God, apparently, before he became the devil.

> Moreover the word of the Lord came unto me, saying, Son of man, take up a lamentation upon the king of Tyrus, and say unto him, Thus saith the Lord God; Thou sealest up the sum, full of wisdom, and perfect in beauty. Thou hast been in Eden the garden of God;

every precious stone was thy covering, the sardius, topaz, and the diamond, the beryl, the onyx, and the jasper, the sapphire, the emerald, and the carbuncle, and gold: the workmanship of thy tabrets and of thy pipes was prepared in thee in the day that thou wast created. Thou art the anointed cherub that covereth; and I have set thee so: thou wast upon the holy mountain of God; thou hast walked up and down in the midst of the stones of fire. Thou wast perfect in thy ways from the day that thou wast created, till iniquity was found in thee. By the multitude of thy merchandise they have filled the midst of thee with violence, and thou hast sinned: therefore I will cast thee as profane out of the mountain of God: and I will destroy thee, O covering cherub, from the midst of the stones of fire. Thine heart was lifted up because of thy beauty, thou hast corrupted thy wisdom by reason of thy brightness: I will cast thee to the ground, I will lay thee before kings, that they may behold thee. Thou hast defiled thy sanctuaries by the multitude of thine iniquities, by the iniquity of thy traffick; therefore will I bring forth a fire from the midst of thee, it shall devour thee, and I will bring thee to ashes upon the earth in the sight of all them that behold thee. All they that know thee among the people shall be astonished at thee: thou shalt be a terror, and never shalt thou be any more.

—Ezekiel 28:11–19

This passage details God's speech to the wicked king of Tyre, who was evidently possessed, indwelled by Satan, as was Judas (John 13:27). So God's Word here, I believe, is directed at Satan. What an indictment. Satan's final destination is Hell.

The Only Way to Avoid Hell

Jesus, who came to save the world, to regenerate mankind by the new birth, talked about Hell more than any other individual. You can find it in the New Testament more than fifty times. He spoke so much about Hell as a warning.

Without Christ, according to the Holy Scriptures, Hell will be your final destination. You will walk through the door of Hell and find yourself in a place of unquenchable fire, torment, and chaos. It will be a place of horror and unspeakable affliction. Everyone should avoid it by believing in Jesus Christ, by accepting Him as Savior and Lord and by coming to God through the blood-bought way of salvation.

You Were Not Meant for Hell

Hell was not created for humans. We read in Matthew's gospel, "Then shall he say also unto them on the left hand, Depart from me, ye cursed, into everlasting fire, prepared for the devil and his angels" (Matthew 25:41). This tells me that God did not prepare Hell or the lake of fire for mankind, but if you follow the devil and his angels, that's where you will surely end up.

Chapter 14

The Great White Throne Judgment

And the devil that deceived them was cast into the lake of fire and brimstone, where the beast and the false prophet are, and shall be tormented day and night for ever and ever.

—Revelation 20:10

The final ruler, the Antichrist, the super deceiver, who will be inhabited by Satan and the ecclesiastical head of the false church, the False Prophet, will not stand before the Great White Throne Judgment. Instead, they will immediately be cast, when the Lord returns, into the lake of fire. There are some who will read this passage and laugh. Thrown into a lake of fire? What a fairy tale, an allegory. Surely a God of love could not do this. And how can one be tormented day and night, forever and ever?

Perhaps you, as a mere man, don't believe this. You say, "It's symbolic. It's allegory. It's myth." But think about it for a moment. Satan and his angels believe. The Bible says, "The devils also believe and tremble" (James 2:19). My friends, if Satan and his angels believe and in believing tremble, should you any less believe? When God says something, He really means it.

The Lake of Fire

At the Great White Throne Judgment, Satan will be judged and cast into the lake of fire with Antichrist and the False Prophet, who've already been there a thousand years. In past years, we have referred to scientific description of Venus, which is very cloudy and very hot—ten thousand degrees Fahrenheit. Scientists have described it as a veritable hellhole—a veritable lake of fire. Other scientists have suggested, as we have talked about black holes, that such a huge, gigantic black hole could be truly, and literally, a lake of fire. Perhaps one of these dark stars will be the destination of Satan and his angels, the Antichrist, the False Prophet, and all who reject Christ and go into eternity without the Lord and without salvation.

A Tragedy

The most tragic moment in all this world and this age is found in Revelation 20:11, which says, "And I saw a great white throne, and him that sat on it, from whose face the earth and the heaven fled away; and there was found no place for them." Apparently, the awesomeness of this occasion is so tragic it is hard for anyone to fully comprehend—the Heaven and the Earth flee away.

You may remember that at the start of the Tribulation period, a throne of judgment was set in Heaven, a Great White Throne.

There was a rainbow round about the throne. Of course, the significance of the rainbow about this throne is that during the seven years of Tribulation judgments, God will show mercy, and many will be saved according to Revelation 7. Genesis 9:11–13 shows the rainbow to be the sign of God's covenant. It is a sign that He will never again destroy all flesh. But to the unbelievers, when their time of judgment comes, God will sit upon His Great White Throne and no rainbow encircles the throne. It will be a fearful occasion, far more frightening than anything man could conjure. The throne is pure white, representing God's absolute holiness. Its glistening whiteness cries out in judgment against all sin and sinners who stand in their darkened state. In their corruptible bodies, there will be no resurrection glory for them.

My dear friends, do you know Jesus as your personal Savior? Do you love Him? Have you said yes? The Bible says that if you will believe in your heart that God raised Jesus from the dead and that He is the anointed of God for sinful man, and you will confess with your mouth the Lord Jesus, you shall be saved. Believe, my friends, in Jesus Christ and live with God in heaven throughout all eternity.

Chapter 15

All Unbelievers Will Go to Hell

The wicked shall be turned into hell, and all the nations that forget God.

—Psalm 9:17

In Psalm 9:17, the Bible tells us graphically, the wicked shall be
turned into Hell and all the nations that forget God. This should
make people everywhere pause and pray for our nation and our
leadership. We should pray for a turning back to God and His Holy
Word.

In the previous chapter, we looked at the Great White Throne
Judgment. This judgment seals the eternal separation of the
unsaved wicked from God. Note that in Revelation 20:13, we are
told that every man was judged according to his works. Keep in
mind that all unbelievers will go to Hell; none will go to Heaven.
Personally, I believe that the people who stand before the Great
White Throne of God will all depart from Him condemned by their

own works and their own words. We read that the books will be opened, and the Book of Life will also be opened, and only those who are found in the Book of Life will go into Heaven (Revelation 20:12). Unbelievers will go to Hell.

Levels of Punishment

While it is true that all unbelievers will go to Hell, it is also true that unbelievers will not receive the same punishment in Hell. Their punishment will be eternal, but the degree of punishment in Hell will vary with every individual. Their punishment will be based according to their works.

> The lord of that servant will come in a day when he looketh not for him, and at an hour when he is not aware, and will cut him in sunder, and will appoint him his portion with the unbelievers. And that servant, which knew his lord's will, and prepared not himself, neither did according to his will, shall be beaten with many stripes. But he that knew not, and did commit things worthy of stripes, shall be beaten with few stripes. For unto whomsoever much is given, of him shall be much required: and to whom men have committed much, of him they will ask the more.
>
> —Luke 12:46–48

Christ relates the truth of the degrees of punishment in Hell through Luke in the form of a parable. The context surrounding this parable is the judgment at the return of Christ, and its purpose is clearly to teach that there will somehow be degrees of punishment in Hell. Both servants represent lost sinners, and both are punished, with neither saved. The intensity of suffering, however, is inflicted based on their degree of sinfulness in relation to the degree of light received or truth known.

Black Holes and the Lake of Fire

In the previous chapter, I mentioned the possibility that Hell could be located within a black hole in space. I would like to explore that more in this chapter. I have read that such a place as the lake of fire is known to science today. The word "lake" must connote a body of matter having liquid form. The planet Jupiter is mostly a gaseous or liquid body. It's mostly composed of helium and hydrogen. Therefore, if Scripture is truth, and I believe it with all my heart, this eternal fire must be in liquid form or in some form in the spirit world that has qualities and characteristics resembling liquid.

The very simple example of the portions of Scripture we're discussing lies in the existence of the singular phenomenon of the skies known as a midget or white dwarf star. A midget star is one which, because of some things which have happened to it should be five thousand or more times as large as it really is, but it has imploded. It has collapsed inwardly, causing a black hole. And when we apply this idea for illustration to such a planet as the Earth, you must conceive the Earth as having shrunk to such an extent that its diameter would be only about four hundred miles instead of eight thousand miles, as it is.

The temperature inside stars that have collapsed in such a way are extremely hot. This enormous density has a great deal to do with our subject. Most people know the sun, our nearest star, is very hot. There's general agreement the temperature near the center of stars is between 25 million and 30 million degrees Fahrenheit. At such temperatures, much can happen. Like the bursting of atoms, which helps to explain the phenomenon of the white dwarf. At such a tremendous temperature, 30 million degrees Fahrenheit, atoms would explode and would lose their electrons even though the attraction between nucleus and electrons is thought to be an octillion times the attraction of gravity. The separated parts could then be better packed in particularly under such great pressure. With the constant activity of X-rays, atom walls could not be reformed. Therefore, enormous densities such as are found in the midgets, can be attained. At such high temperatures, all matter would be in the form of gas in a white dwarf. The pressure would be so great that the gas would become compressed to the consistency of a liquid.

These midget stars can never cool off. Before such a star could cool off and gradually become dark like a black hole, it would have to expand to normal proportions. It would have to get to be more than five thousand time its present size, and therein lies the difficulty. Such expansion would cause enormous heat, which in turn would absolutely keep the star compressed. So, in as far as astronomers and physicists know, midget stars can never cool off. You talk about a fire and brimstone that burns forever? Well, it's scientifically possible. The white dwarf can never burn out.

And they shall go forth, and look upon the carcases of the men that have transgressed against me: for their worm shall not die, neither shall their fire be quenched; and they shall be an abhorring unto all flesh.

—Isaiah 66:24

In Isaiah 66:24, we find an eternal fire which cannot burn out. A white dwarf cannot be quenched. Any quenching material such as water would immediately have its atom stripped of electrons and be packed in with the rest. It would get even hotter. Although we cannot say that God will actually use white dwarfs to fulfill His Word, the answer to the skeptic is in the heavens. Since black holes exist, there is such a thing as a lake of fire.

Chapter 16

Hell Is a Real Place

And the sea gave up the dead which were in it; and death and hell delivered up the dead which were in them: and they were judged every man according to their works. And death and hell were cast into the lake of fire. This is the second death. And whosoever was not found written in the book of life was cast into the lake of fire.

—Revelation 20:13–15

Now, in the Bible, in Revelation, the final book of the New Testament, we read this spine-chilling passage. The only way I can understand this passage is that there is a fallen spirit being or spirit prince who is over the domain of death and also the region of Hell. When it says death and hell were cast in lake of fire, it's not simply a compartment, it is an entity, a spirit being. I feel like I can really prove that or establish it.

"Destruction and death say, We have heard the fame thereof with our ears" (Job 28:22). In Job 28:22 we read about destruction and death. These are the principalities or the princes who are over death and hell. They say, "We have heard the fame thereof with our ears." Of course, they are talking about wisdom. Where does wisdom come from? Of course, we know it comes from God and God is a fountain in the source of all wisdom.

Then we finish Revelation 20 with, "And whosoever was not found written in the book of life was cast into the lake of fire." Possibly, maybe the entire tremendous crowd that stands before our Savior, Jesus Christ, the Son of God, when He sits upon the Great White Throne, and He judges this great host out of the record books and the Book of Life.

The Bible tells us that Hell is a prepared place. It is a real place. It is a real torment. However, it was not meant to be a place for mankind. In Matthew 25:41, Jesus said, "Depart from me, ye cursed, into everlasting fire, prepared for the devil and his angels." Then Jesus said, "And these shall go away into everlasting punishment: but the righteous into life eternal" (Matthew 25:46). The word "prepared" literally means "having been prepared." This suggests that the lake of fire is already in existence. I believe it is possible that Hell could be in a tremendous black hole, which is already in existence awaiting their occupants.

The Rich Man and Lazarus

Hell will be a place of conscious, eternal torment. Remember the story in Luke 16 about the rich man who died and went to Hell. Now, some people say, "Well, this is a parable. This is not a real story." But there was a real rich man and there was a real beggar named Lazarus. And I believe it was not a parable, but a very literal and real story.

There was a certain rich man, which was clothed in purple and fine linen, and fared sumptuously every day: And there was a certain beggar named Lazarus, which was laid at his gate, full of sores, And desiring to be fed with the crumbs which fell from the rich man's table: moreover the dogs came and licked his sores. And it came to pass, that the beggar died, and was carried by the angels into Abraham's bosom: the rich man also died, and was buried; And in hell he lift up his eyes, being in torments, and seeth Abraham afar off, and Lazarus in his bosom. And he cried and said, Father Abraham, have mercy on me, and send Lazarus, that he may dip the tip of his finger in water, and cool my tongue; for I am tormented in this flame. But Abraham said, Son, remember that thou in thy lifetime receivedst thy good things, and likewise Lazarus evil things: but now he is comforted, and thou art tormented. And beside all this, between us and you there is a great gulf fixed: so that they which would pass from hence to you cannot; neither can they pass to us, that would come from thence. Then he said, I pray thee therefore, father, that thou wouldest send him to my father's house: For I have five brethren; that he may testify unto them, lest they also come into this place of torment. Abraham saith unto him, They have Moses and the prophets; let them hear them. And he said, Nay, father Abraham: but if one went unto them from the dead, they will repent. And he said unto him, If they hear not Moses and the prophets, neither will they be persuaded, though one rose from the dead.

—Luke 16:19–31

Notice the Bible says that the rich man was in Hades or Hell, the realm of the dead. He was in torment, and he lifted up his eyes and cried out. So even though he was out of the body, he was still a real person. He still had eyes and he still had a mouth by which he could cry out.

The scripture indicates the unsaved dead are conscious. My dear friends, do not believe the talk about soul sleep. You will not sleep when your body dies and you depart this life. You will be just as conscious as you are today, but your soul and spirit will leave the dead body, for God has decreed that a living being cannot stay in a dead body. When you depart your dead body, your soul and your spirit will go to be with God or you will go to the lower regions of the Earth, a place of great heat, a place of torment, and a place of darkness as darkness itself.

The Fires of Hell

Notice also that the rich man asked Abraham to send Lazarus to warn his five brothers lest they too come into this place of torment. So, we have many indications from God that Hell is a real place of torment. It is a literal place. It is also shown from this passage in Luke 16 to be a hot place. The rich man said that he was tormented in the flame. It was an actual flame. It was real torment. He wanted just a little drop of water to cool his tongue for he was in torment.

Can you imagine the intense suffering from the unbearable heat? Anyone who has been to Vietnam or other hot climates or the Persian Gulf where the suffocating humidity envelopes you along with intense heat, can appreciate this scene. Or if you have been to Death Valley in Arizona or visited the Dead Sea in Israel, the lowest place on the face of the Earth, you know about the intense heat and humidity. Picture the desperateness of this occasion. When the rich man would welcome the beggar Lazarus (whom I'm sure he looked upon with contempt in his life) to get a little water on his finger to alleviate his suffering just a little. My friend, Hell is truly a place of real torment.

The Darkness of Hell

We are also told that Hell is a place of darkness. In Matthew, the unsaved will be driven out in a darkness where there will be weeping and gnashing of teeth. Jesus said the lost, "... shall be cast out into outer darkness: there shall be weeping and gnashing of teeth." Think about for a moment. If you are an unbeliever and some of your best friends, your husband, your wife are believers, they will go to Heaven, and you will be eternally separated from them in total darkness.

In Job 10, the last two verses, I believe Job with the inspiration of God, gives us a description of what Hell is like.

> Before I go whence I shall not return, even to the land of darkness and the shadow of death; A land of darkness, as darkness itself; and of the shadow of death, without any order, and where the light is as darkness.
>
> —Job 10:21–22

Hell is a land of darkness, is darkness itself, and of the shadow of death without any order and where the light is as darkness. To me, this is a picture of a place that is so dark even the light in it is darkness, where there is no order, only tumult and chaos. And of course, when Job is talking about going to such a place, he's talking about the fact that Abraham's bosom was on one side of the lower region of the Earth with a great chasm between, and then the place of darkness and intense heat.

My dear friend, believe the gospel. Receive Jesus Christ as your personal Savior and Lord and know that there is a Hell to shun and a Heaven to gain by your all-important decision.

As awesome as Heaven will be for those who accept Jesus Christ as their Savior, Hell will be that much more awful for those who reject Him. One cannot read the Bible seriously without seeing it repeatedly—the line is drawn. The Bible says there is one and only one way to Heaven—Jesus Christ. Follow the Lord's command: "Enter ye in at the strait gate: for wide is the gate, and broad is the way, that leadeth to destruction, and many there be which go in thereat: Because strait is the gate, and narrow is the way, which leadeth unto life, and few there be that find it" (Matthew 7:13–14). Faith in Jesus is the one means of going to Heaven. Those who have faith are guaranteed to get there. Do you trust in Jesus?

Will you actually enter God's Kingdom? How can you guarantee that you will go to Heaven? The Bible makes a clear distinction between those who have eternal life and those who do not: "He that hath the Son hath life; and he that hath not the Son of God hath not life" (1 John 5:12). It all goes back to faith. Those who believe in Christ are made the children of God (John 1:12). Those who accept Jesus' sacrifice as the payment for their sins and who believe in His resurrection are going to Heaven. Those who reject Christ are not. "He that believeth on him is not condemned: but he that believeth not is condemned already, because he hath not believed in the name of the only begotten Son of God" (John 3:18).

So, which will it be? Heaven? Or Hell? The choice is yours …

How to Receiver Jesus Christ

1. Admit your need (I am a sinner).
2. Be willing to turn from your sins (repent).
3. Believe that Jesus died for you and rose from the grave
4. Through prayer, invite Jesus Christ to come in and control your life through the Holy Spirit (receive Him as Lord and Savior).

What to Pray

Dear Lord Jesus,

I know that I am a sinner and I need Your forgiveness. I believe that You died for my sins. I want to turn from my sins. I now invite You to come into my heart and life. I want to trust and follow You as Lord and Savior.

In Jesus' Name, Amen.

The Great Pyramid
Prophecy in Stone

The Scriptures say that God established wonders in the land of Egypt.

» When was the Great Pyramid built?

» Who was the builder?

» Why was it built?

These are questions that continue to be debated by archaeologists, astronomers, other scientists, and historians. As brought out by the author, there is evidence that the Great Pyramid also incorporates a prophetic timetable for coming events, including the coming Tribulation and the return of Jesus Christ.

Get your copy today
1(800) 652-1144 | www.swrc.com

More Faith-Building Books from Beacon Street Press

» **Prayers of the Ancients** by Kenneth C. Hill—How did people like Daniel, David, and Moses talk to God? What can we learn from their example? Your prayer life will be enriched as you study the greatest prayers in the Bible.

» **By God's Grace: A Cancer Survivor's Testimony** by Vaughn Shatzer—This life-changing story is an encouragement to everyone. Learn how the fiery trial of cancer brought the Shatzer family to a new level of trust, faith, patience, and hope in God.

» **Jewish Roots of Christianity** by Larry Stamm—In this biblical survey, Larry Stamm, a first-generation Holocaust survivor and Jewish follower of Jesus, examines the religion of the Old Testament and its ultimate fulfillment in Jesus Christ.

» **The Shepherd** by James Collins—In *The Shepherd*, James Collins teaches the 23rd Psalm verse-by-verse, explaining its extraordinary power to change lives. This book will help you rediscover the joy, inspiration, and peace of this beloved psalm.

» **Panorama of Creation** by Carl Baugh—Mankind's greatest battle, creation vs. evolution, is before us. Dr. Baugh scientifically proves that special creation is the only explanation for man's existence on this planet. Bonus chapter on dinosaurs.

» **The Power of the Cross** by Robert Lindsted—In *The Power of the Cross*, Dr. Lindsted teaches through the trial, crucifixion, and resurrection of Jesus Christ. Discover the significance of the seven sayings from the cross.

» ***Living in Today's World*** by Greg Patten—Greg shares timeless tales filled with compassion and love that are guaranteed to minister to multiple generations. Have your soul encouraged with these uplifting stories of *Living in Today's World*.

Get your copy today
1(800) 652-1144 | www.swrc.com